W9-CKM-129

THE WOMEN AT POINT SUR

THE WOMEN AT POINT SUR

AND OTHER POEMS

BY

ROBINSON JEFFERS

AFTERWORD BY TIM HUNT

NEW YORK
LIVERIGHT
1977

Copyright © 1977 by Liveright Publishing Corporation
Copyright 1927 by R. Jeffers, copyright 1955 by Robinson
Jeffers
Published simultaneously in Canada by George J. McLeod
Limited, Toronto. Printed in the United States of America.

"Soliloquy" is reprinted from *The Selected Poetry of Robinson Jeffers*. Copyright 1938 and renewed 1966 by Donnan Jeffers and Garth Jeffers. Reprinted by permission of Random House, Inc.

Library of Congress Cataloging in Publication Data

Jeffers, Robinson, 1887–1962.
    The women at Point Sur and other poems.

    I. Title.
PS3519.E27W6   1977   811'.5'2   76–55798
ISBN 0–87140–626–8
ISBN 0–87140–115–0 pbk.

1 2 3 4 5 6 7 8 9 0

94358

CONTENTS

THE WOMEN AT POINT SUR

PRELUDE

I drew solitude over me, on the lone shore,
By the hawk-perch stones; the hawks and the gulls
   are never breakers of solitude.
When the animals Christ was rumored to have died for
   drew in,
The land thickening, drew in about me, I planted trees
   eastward, and the ocean
Secured the west with the quietness of thunder. I was
   quiet.
Imagination, the traitor of the mind, has taken my soli-
   tude and slain it.
No peace but many companions; the hateful-eyed
And human-bodied are all about me: you that love
   multitude may have them.

But why should I make fables again? There are many
Tellers of tales to delight women and the people.
I have no vocation. The old rock under the house, the
   hills with their hard roots and the ocean hearted
With sacred quietness from here to Asia
Make me ashamed to speak of the active little bodies,
   the coupling bodies, the misty brainfuls
Of perplexed passion. Humanity is needless.
I said, "Humanity is the start of the race, the gate to
   break away from, the coal to kindle,
The blind mask crying to be slit with eye-holes."
Well, now it is done, the mask slit, the rag burnt, the
   starting-post left behind: but not in a fable.

Culture's outlived, art's root-cut, discovery's
The way to walk in.   Only remains to invent the lan-
    guage to tell it.   Match-ends of burnt experience
Human enough to be understood,
Scraps and metaphors will serve.   The wine was a little
    too strong for the new wine-skins . . .

                                    Come storm, kind storm.
Summer and the days of tired gold
And bitter blue are more ruinous.
The leprous grass, the sick forest,
The sea like a whore's eyes,
And the noise of the sun,
The yellow dog barking in the blue pasture,
Snapping sidewise.
                        When I remembered old rains,
Running clouds and the iron wind, then the trees
    trembled.
I was calling one of the great dancers
Who wander down from the Aleutian rocks and the
    open Pacific,
Pivoting counter-sunwise, celebrating power with the
    whirl of a dance, sloping to the mainland.
I watched his feet waken the water
And the ocean break in foam beyond Lobos;
The iron wind struck from the hills.
                            You are tired and corrupt,
You kept the beast under till the fountain's poisoned,
He drips with mange and stinks through the oubliette
    window.
The promise-breaker war killed whom it freed,
And none living's the cleaner.   Yet storm comes, the
    lions hunt

In the nights striped with lightning. It will come: feed
    on peace
While the crust holds: to each of you at length a little
Desolation; a pinch of lust or a drop of terror:
Then the lions hunt in the brain of the dying: storm is
    good, storm is good, good creature,
Kind violence, throbbing throat aches with pity.
                                        Onorio Vasquez,
Young seer of visions who lives with his six brothers
On the breast of Palo Corona mountain looking north-
    ward,
Watches his brother Vidal and Julio the youngest
Play with a hawk they shot from the mountain cloud,
The wing broken. They crucified the creature,
A nail in the broken wing on the barn wall
Between the pink splinters of bone and a nail in the
    other.
They prod his breast with a wand, no sponge of vinegar,
"Fly down, Jew-beak." The wind streams down the
    mountain,
The river of cloud streams over: Onorio Vasquez
Never sees anything to the point. What he sees:
The ocean like sleek gray stone perfectly jointed
To the heads and bays, a woman walking upon it,
The curling scud of the storm around her ankles,
Naked and strong, her thighs the height of the moun-
    tain, walking and weeping,
The shadow of hair under the belly, the jutting breasts
    like hills, the face in the hands and the hair
Streaming north. "Why are you sad, our lady?" "I
    had only one son.
The strange lover never breaks the window-latches again
When Joseph's at synagogue."

[11]

                    Orange eyes, tired and fierce,
They're casting knives at you now, but clumsily, the
    knives
Quiver in the wood, stern eyes the storm deepens.
Don't wince, topaz eyes.
                The wind wearies toward evening,
Old Vasquez sends his boys to burn the high pastures
Against the rain: see the autumn fires on the mountain,
    creeping red lakes and crescents
Up the black slope in the slide of the year: that's Vas-
    quez and his boys burning the mountain. The high
    wind
Holds, the low dies, the black curtain flies north.
                       Myrtle Cartwright
Locked the windows but forgot the door, it's a lonely
    canyon
When the waves flap in the creek-mouth. Andrew's
    driving
The calves to Monterey, he trusts her, he doesn't know
How all her flesh burned with lascivious desire
Last year, but she remembered her mother and prayed
And God quenched it. Prayer works all right: three
    times
Rod Stewart came down to see her, he might have been
    wood
For all she cared. She suffers with constipation,
Tired days and smothering dreams, she's young, life's
    cheerless,
God sent a little sickness to keep her decent
Since the great prayer. What's that in the west,
    thunder?
The sea rumbles like thunder but the wind's died down,
Soon it should rain.

Myrtle Cartwright
Could sleep if her heart would quit moving the bed-
    clothes;
The lighthouse-keeper's daughter little Faith Heriot
Says, "Father the cow's got loose, I must go out
With the storm coming and bring her into the stable.
What would mother do without milk in the morning?"
(Clearly Point Pinos light: stands back from the sea
Among the rolling dunes cupped with old pasture.
Nobody'd keep a cow on the rock at Point Sur.)
This girl never goes near the cowshed but wanders
Into the dunes, the long beam of the light
Swims over and over her head in the high darkness,
The spray of the storm strains through the beam but
    Faith
Crouches out of the wind in a hollow of the sand
And hears the sea, she rolls on her back in the clear sand
Shuddering, and feels the light lie thwart her hot body
And the sand trickle into the burning places
Comes pale to the house: "Ah, Bossy led me a chase,
Led me a chase." The lighthouse-keeper believes in hell,
His daughter's wild for a lover, his wife sickening to-
    ward cancer,
The long yellow beam wheels over the wild sea and the
    strain
Gathers in the air.
                    Oh crucified
Wings, orange eyes, open?
Always the strain, the straining flesh, who feels what
    God feels
Knows the straining flesh, the aching desires,
The enormous water straining its bounds, the electric
Strain in the cloud, the strain of the oil in the oil-
    tanks

At Monterey, aching to burn, the strain of the spinning
Demons that make an atom, straining to fly asunder,
Straining to rest at the center,
The strain in the skull, blind strains, force and counter-
    force,
Nothing prevails . . .
        Oh, in storm: storm's kind, kind violence,
When the swollen cloud ached—suddenly
Her charge and agony condensed, slip, the thick dark
Whelps lightning; the air breaks, the twin birth rain
    falls globed
From the released blackness high up in the air
Ringing like a bell for deliverance.
            Many-folded hills
Mouth the black voice that follows the white eye
Opening, universal white eye widening and shut. Myrtle
    Cartwright's
One of those whom thunder shakes with terror: head
    covered
Against the flashes: "If it should find me and kill me
What's life been worth? Nothing, nothing, nothing,
    death's horrible."
She hears it like a truck driven jolting through heaven
Rumble to the north. "And if I die old:
Nothing, nothing."
       Vasquez' boys have gone home.
                Deep after
    midnight the wind rises, turns iron again,
From east of south, it grinds the heads of the hills, the
    dunes move in the dark at Point Pinos, the sand-
    stone
Lighthouse at Point Sur on the top of the rock is like
    an axhead held against a grindstone.
The high redwoods have quit roaring to scream. Oaks

go down on the mountain. At Vasquez' place in
the yellow
Pallor of dawn the roof of the barn's lifting, his sons
cast ropes over the timbers. The crucified
Snaps his beak at them. He flies on two nails.
Great eyes, lived all night?
Onorio should have held the rope but it slid through his
fingers. Onorio Vasquez
Never sees anything to the point. What he sees:
The planted eucalyptuses bent double
All in a row, praying north, "Why everything's praying
And running northward, old hawk anchored with nails
You see that everything goes north like a river.
On a cliff in the north
Stands the strange lover, shines and calls."

                                              In the morning
The inexhaustible clouds flying up from the south
Stream rain, the gullies of the hills grow alive, the
creeks flood, the summer sand-bars
Burst from their mouths, from every sea-mouth wedges
of yellow, yellow tongues. Myrtle Cartwright
Hears the steep cataracts slacken, and then thunder
Pushes the house-walls. "Hear me, God, death's not
dreadful.
You heard before when I prayed. Now," she whispers,
"I'll make the bargain," thunder leans on the house-
walls, "life's no value
Like this, I'm going to Stewart's, I can't live empty.
Now Andrew can't come home for every canyon
Vomits its bridge, judgment is yours only,
Death's in your hands." She opens the door on the
streaming
Canyon-side, the desperate wind: the dark wet oak-
leaves

All in a moment each leaf a distinct fire
Reflects the sharp flash over them: Myrtle Cartwright
Feels the sword plunge: no touch: runs tottering up hill
Through the black voice.

                    Black pool of oil hidden in the oil-tank
In Monterey felt the sword plunge: touched: the wild
    heat
Went mad where a little air was, metal curled back,
Fire leaped at the outlet. "Immense ages
We lay under rock, our lust hoarded,
The ache of ignorant desire, the enormous pressure,
The enormous patience, the strain, strain, the strain
Lightened we lay in a steel shell . . . what God kept
    for us:
Roaring marriage."

                  Myrtle Cartwright wins up hill
    through the oak-scrub
And through the rain, the wind at the summit
Knocks her breasts and her mouth, she crouches in the
    mud,
Feels herself four-foot like a beast and the lightning
Will come from behind and cover her, the wolf of white
    fire,
Force the cold flesh, cling with his forepaws. "Oh,
    death's
What I was after." She runs on the road northward,
    the wind behind her,
The lightnings like white doves hovering her head, harm-
    less as pigeons, through great bars of black noise.
She lifts her wet arms. "Come, doves."

                        The oil-tank boils
    with joy in the north, one among ten, one tank
Burns, the nine others wait, feel warmth, dim change of
    patience. This one roars with fulfilled desire,

[16]

The ring-bound molecules splitting, the atoms dancing
    apart, marrying the air.

                            Myrtle Cartwright

Knocks on her door: "Oh, I've come. Here's what you
    wanted." (In the yellow inland no rain but the
    same lightning,
And it lights a forest.) He leads her into the barn
    because there are people in the house.

                      In the north the oil-tanks

Catch from the first, the ring-bound molecules splitting,
    the atoms dancing apart, marrying the air.
The marriage bound thighs opening, on the stiff white
    straw, the nerves of fire, the ganglia like stars.

Don't you see any vision Onorio Vasquez? "No, for
    the topazes
Have dulled out of his head, he soars on two nails,
Dead hawk over the coast. Oh little brother
Julio, if you could drive nails through my hands
I'd stand against the door: through the middle of the
    palms:
And take the hawk's place, you could throw knives at me.
I'd give you my saddle and the big bridle, Julio,
With the bit that rings and rings when the horse twirls
    it."
He smiles. "You'd see the lights flicker in my hair."
He smiles craftily. "You'd live long and be rich,
And nobody could beat you in running or riding."
He chatters his teeth. "It is necessary for someone to
    be fastened with nails.
And Jew-beak died in the night. Jew-beak is dead."

THE WOMEN AT POINT SUR

I

The Rev. Dr. Barclay outgrew his profession,
He stood on the platform, his hands like wires in a
    wind, silent, the eyes coals
In the dead face. "I have nothing for you." The face
    began twitching, he felt it. "I have something to
    tell you.
This place is dead, it is dead." He saw the narrow
    face of Audis his wife shine white by his child's.
"I am not a poor man, I haven't hung by the salary. I
    have served here ten years, I have made great
    friendships, I've honestly
Done what I thought was due. The creed died in my
    mind, I kept the pastorate, I thought the spirit,
The revolutionary spirit of Christ would survive, flame
    the more freely. There are many others
Leaders of churches have sunk the myths and swim by
    the ethic. Love: and not resist violence: which one
    of us
Holds to that now? Dared name it this time last year?"
    The assistant pastor
Was present, and suddenly standing in the aisle: "Dr.
    Barclay is ill.
The long strain of his pastorate, his labors and bereave-
    ment: he must rest . . ." But Barclay twitching his
    head, the lean face

Like white fire in the dimness through the colored windows: "I am well, and enough rested, this dim air
Has heard enough lies." The other one still attempting to speak, "Sit down, will you, I am not patient."
And he said to the people: "You are kindly and simple, you made war when they told you to, you have made peace when they told you.
You obey the laws, you are simple people, you love authority. *I* have authority
Here, and no man will hinder me while I make my confession. I have been a blind man leading you blind.
Nobody can build the truth on lies. My blindness is not removed.
I have nothing true to tell you, no profession but ignorance, I can tell you what's false. Christianity is false.
The fable that Christ was the son of God and died to save you, died and lived again. Lies. You'd swallow
The yarns of idle fishermen, the wash of Syria? You are very simple people. It is time to scour off.
I tell you," he said: but the people were all moving, the great pipes of the organ
Poured into voice behind him, sonorous and ordered
Storm-fall roaring his words down, "repent, repent. Repent," through loops and moments of the noise they heard him
Crying, words glittered like hands through a net, having no meaning. Men moved in the aisles, Barclay remembered
The electric switchboard back of the platform, he strode to the back, threw the main switch, the organ groaned silent

[20]

Like a shot beast. Three men had mounted the plat-
form steps, and Barclay
Fiercely and suddenly: "Go down, I am here:" they
wavered backward
Unsure, shrinking from violence; they found the steps
and went down. Barclay above them:
"Listen but once. To hear me again you'll have to
follow me. Thought is not easy, I am giving you
ten years'
Thought in a moment's words. It is not possible
To know anything while you eat lies: you half-believers,
fog-people: leave that, wash the eyes, and who
knows
Now the earth draws to maturity, has taken the bloody
Initiation of coming of age, you also grown adult
May fish some flaming gleam of knowledge out of the
netted ocean, run down some deer of perception
In the dark wood: certainly it is hopeless, oh desperate;
no man
Down all the blind millenniums has known anything, no,
not a scrap, not a dust-grain: I am calling you to
that
Blind adventure, I call you to take despair by the throat:
I know you are fools and soft, woman-brained,
I have lived among you, I have held my mouth not to
despise you: I would set the sheep on the wolves
to this end,
The doves at the hawk's nest . . . It is no alliance
And I am the hunter you shall not run as hounds for:
but think, you old men, you old women, if one of you
Should stumble over it by chance, you had cleaned the
mind that you could see it, some instant pebble
of perception

[21]

Glowing in the dust.   Tell me if you find it, I am going
    away
And give the tag-end of my life to that purpose," he
    said quietly; and cried out
"I have been on the verge, these years.   You with your
    monkey hubbub crossed me when I touched it.
When it lay in my hands: you with your marriages and
    your burials, your newspapers, the noise you keep
    up
Under the stars, your national quarrels and your ob-
    servances,
Flags, fireworks, songs to dead Gods: from moment to
    moment
While it knocked for entrance.   I am going off alone
    and gather my mind, I have something fiery
Here that will burn the world down to significance."
    The aisle opened for him
Going down from the platform, passing alone to the
    doors.

II

He went alone to the vacation cottage near Monterey,
Thence wandered southward the coast.   On the road
     crossing Sovranes Canyon despair covered him like
     water.
"I have broken my life like a dry stick and have come
     no nearer, in the city when I raged against time
It seemed in hand's reach."   He thought of the house
     he had lived in.   "Not that.   Sticks plastered, cloth,
     books, what they call a home;
Framed to wall out the wild face of eternity."
He thought of Audis his wife.   "Not her.   If it were
     possible
I'd not go back there."   He seemed to have passed into
     a vacuum, no means, no resistance, valueless free-
     dom
Like a vain ghost's in the air.   Nothing solid, the roots
     out.   He climbed the small steep hill by the road,
He struck his hands against the rocks at the peak, the
     knuckles were bleeding: "All this energy to waste.
I am fifty years old and have this energy."   The tide
     of high excitement returned, he unconscious of it,
Rising by waves.   "Certainly I shall put out my hands
     and touch power.   He is here, he is here."   The
     sea's tide
Rose too, white-sheeting the dark reefs at the rock-foot,
     in the dark south the domed rock at Point Sur

[23]

Stood opposite the mainland wall of hills; clouds closed
the sea-line; landward far down the hill-slope a
hawk
Hung like a wind-vane, motionless with beating wings
in the stream of the wind. A man tethered his
mount
To the fence beneath it. Dr. Barclay felt in his fore-
head behind the eyes the ache of stored force
Beating against the sockets of the eyes. "When it finds
release, when it finds it . . .
The vulture's got the sky of the hawk: you, brain, this
power
Throngs you will not break through? There is a power
behind the appearances, you will break through to
it and touch it.
Death's got the sky of the vulture: the flaw in the story.
Fifty years old, facing the desperate . . . I shall not
die blind. Jesus did: 'why hast thou forsaken me,
my God?'
I not his son take him by violence. This is that hybris
in the tragedy, that brings destruction.
Content. I will buy." It came to him like a whisper
from outward: "Plow the air, what harvest: take the
earth in your hands.
God thinks through action, how shall a man but through
action?" "I have cut myself off, I acted when I
cut myself off
From action: I am only a wandering mind reaching at
knowledge." But he thought "It is true that I have
reached nothing.
The presence I almost touched in the crowds . . . what
was it I sought? . . . that came in flashes, vanishes
derisive

[24]

When the eyes focus. To mould one's thoughts from
    action. Give up sanity again, be mad enough to
    act.
This fellow that climbs up the hill to prick my solitude:
Kill him and hide the body, that would be action, not
    an inch more monstrous
Than any other. I cannot think what it was that I
    was trying to discover, to find out something,
I wrote it on paper yesterday. Here it is: Oh, these:
First, whether there's any . . . what the vulgar call
    God . . . spirit of the universe.
But spirit's a more contaminated word than the other.
    Life then, one life
Informing . . . no, being: whether it's one being . . .
    why, this is evident.
Second, is anything left after we die but worm's meat?
    Third, how should men live?
I have something to solve!
                              You want to speak to me?"
"Yes sir: you're Dr. Barclay? A letter for you."
"From Mrs. Barclay?" He read. "Have you got a
    knife, my pencil's broken.
Young man, I'm curious to know what people believe.
Do you think there's a God?" He stared; and Barclay:
    "You think so:
You're ashamed to say so. What have we preachers
    done, how have we slandered him,
That people are ashamed to speak of him without laugh-
    ing?
Must clean our conceptions. Well, it's true, there is one.
If you define the word.
But the oyster wonders whether his element's conscious,
The great night-cored and storm-striped. You have no
    opinion?"

[25]

"I haven't." "The letter? It's absurd not to know
  anything.
You choose to ignore consciousness, incredible how
    quickly
The American mind short-circuits by ignoring its object.
Something in the gelded air of the country. Tell Mrs.
    Barclay,
No need of writing, if she pleases may follow me.
Do you know whether my daughter's with her, a girl
Twenty years old? Oh, you'd have noticed.
I shall have to do something, God thinks through action
And all this show is God's brain, the water, the cloud
    yonder,
The coast hills, thinking the thing out to conclusion.
Tell her that I'm walking southward.

It is certain," he thought after the man had gone down,
"The mind's powerless in vacuo, no one can dispense
    with disciples
And burn to the essence.
Those are the birds that are not caught but with confi-
    dence.
What's honesty, the end is honest. I should have taken
    him.
He serves the hotel, he is not proper to this earth
I shall crop the pure fruit of. If I must."

III

Going down he felt a dizziness, he stumbled, and the
 world
Dissolved in a moment.   After a moment's error in the
 gulf of emptiness
He leaned and touched the hill with his hand, he modelled
 with his hand room enough to crouch on, and
 slowly,
Painfully, element by element, summoned the world
 back.
Willed it to being, and with the pain of creation.
Walked in his made world: some minutes that followed
Each footfall needed thought and creation to plant itself
 on
For the gaps in the dim fabric.
                              He stopped at a farm-
 house about sundown,
Bought food.   The woman was severe and suspicious;
Not knowing what incredible guest . . . "I keep my
 secret,
I hide myself in the body of an old man.
Why should I be troubled with praise and thanksgiving?"

IV

The moon had stood on the hills like a domed mountain
Before sundown; he had walked in the night and slept
    by the roadside.
He remembered on a silver headland over black abysses
A multitude of people had followed him; he had stood
On raised ground by the roadside: "Oh faithful-hearted
The change of the world has come indeed and you do
    wisely to follow me.
Nevertheless the seed is not ripe. I am gathering seed
    in a great solitude, I shall tell you everything
When I return, but not now. These little ones would
    faint on the way, it is far and you cannot follow
    me."
He had left them there. He remembered enormous
    descents into the darkness,
Interminable climbs through the rank night of the red-
    woods
On the north slopes.
                He brushed his clothing at dawn,
And washed when he found water. At a prosperous
    farmhouse
Lodging was refused him, he went on southward
And saw from the road over the great bronze height
Eastward the mountain Pico Blanco, westward the rock
    at Point Sur crowned with its lighthouse
Against great waters; a gated way dropped seaward,

[28]

He followed, he came to the gaunt farmhouse that stood
High over gap-roofed barns and broken wagons;
They had told him he might be given lodging at Mor-
head's.
High cube-shaped house, redwood logs squared and
jointed,
Blackened with ancient weathers, chinked with white
plaster,
Striped like a zebra with the white plaster, and the
porch
Rotting under its rose-vine.
      The young woman at the door
Needed persuasion, but now his mind was so clear
After the night's bewilderment, he understood
Perfectly. Her husband not yet back from the army,
The ranch was too much to manage, they were very poor
And lived poorly. Indeed the price of his lodging
Would help toward paying the cowboy.
      He thought, could he hire a horse
For Edward to ride? Edward was dead.
"My boy was only eighteen, he was killed in France
Two years ago." She answered, "My Rachel's four.
She had a fever two years ago." She took him up-
stairs
Through the dark house and showed him the room.
He lived there quietly, feeling the strings and tendons
Of his mind mend; he seemed remembering the sources,
The causes; he walked on the hillside over the great
sand-flat
And the burnished ocean.
      The storms in his mind had
had their signal,
When he had imagined, O corrupt fool, too near a
friendship . . .

Should they not love each other, they were born twins.
That anger of his when Edward before his departure
Locked himself in the room with April to bid her fare-
   well:
He had paced the hallway below, his mind boiling,
And suffered like a fainting-fit or a dizziness:
Sorrow at his son's departure: annihilating the world
A moment or more.
                    Annihilation, the beautiful
Word, the black crystal structure, prisms of black crystal
Arranged the one behind the other in the word
To catch a ray not of this world.
                              Was it possible
His outburst against religion, against his ministry,
Dated from there, the public passionate resentment?
No; that was reasoned; having taught falsehoods,
   countenanced
Lies, must denounce them publicly. And the death of
   his son
Involved in the same texture; his own starved impotent
Desert of years.
                  Six came to table in the house.
Himself, and Mrs. Morhead; the four-year-old
Rachel her child; two farmhands; and the girl Faith
   Heriot
Who was certainly friend not servant, relative perhaps,
Of Mrs. Morhead's, and nursed the old cripple upstairs
On the third floor, under the roof: old Morhead,
The absent husband's father, the owner of the farm
Probably; but never came down, sepulchred in bed
Under the roof while the place drifted to ruin.

What were they doing in the nights? No doubt the
   old cripple

Was restless, the girl Faith Heriot would move over-
    head
Barefoot or softly slippered; and she or another
Steal up and down the creaking stairs in the dark.

V

The fourth day of his lodging at Morhead's his mind
Was quieter, he wrote a brief letter to his wife.
"Dear Audis my mind is quieter. I repent nothing,
It was my duty to protest publicly.
I shall live here some months quieting my mind."
He was directing the bank to set to her account
(Three quarters, scored through and erased) one half
　　his income
Monthly, enough, he thought, to keep up the house
For April and herself. And his love, he added,
To herself and April.
　　　　　　　　He wrote to the bank also.
A man would drive to the stage-road in the afternoon
And post them for him.
　　　　　　　　It was too easy to be at peace,
　　quieting the mind.
Easily he could live here forever and build up peace
　　like a fortress. "For this I have broken—to be
　　quiet—
My life like a dry stick? That's to feed fire with."
　　He hurried from the house and went up
Toward the bronze hills. "Die blind, die ignorant?"
　　Ever at remembering that he was fifty years old
　　it pierced him
With stammering hurry and precipitance. He walked
　　on the hill like one carrying a torch in the wind on
　　the hillside,

Seeking and seeking, the smoke and the flame blowing
    up the gray gullies, twisted and flaring,
Nothing, nothing found. He sat in unbearable dejection
On the open starved earth. The power was all drained.
There was a time he had felt it in the skull
Like molten iron pushing for outlet.
Now emptiness, like a band over the coronal suture the
    ache of the emptiness
In the bone vault below. Some buzzing arrowlets like
    stray electrons
In the void of space, gnats under a vault. Annihilation
Is the most beautiful word. "Edward, my son,
Feeds on the fruit of that bough."
He pushed his hand palm forward from the face out-
    ward.
"I will not touch peace." He rose and being for the
    time hopeless
Turned from himself, there was no help in that empti-
    ness.
He saw over the triangle-shaped sand-flat the great
    black rock of Point Sur against the blue water.
His mind relieved of vigilance instantly told him:
God thinks through action. There are only two ways:
    gather disciples
To fling like bullets against God and discover him:
Or else commit an act so monstrous, so irreparable
It will stand like a mountain of rock, serve you for
    fulcrum
To rest the lever. In vacancy: nothing." He imagined
A priest by the yet-twitching carcass of sacrifice
Plunging his hands into the hot red cavern
Through the cut ribs and midriff, dragging out the
    heart,
Lifting it to the God of the sky, the thick blood

Rains on his face. "What is man? The filthiest of
　　beasts;
But a discoverer, God sprouted him for the sake of dis-
　　covery.
I have voyaged outside the maps, these waters not
　　charted,"
He said exultantly. Going down the hill a company
　　followed him,
His daughter April among them. "Do you love me,
　　April?"
"Dearest!" "I am going to war, we must be alone for
　　farewell.
The people press me.—I have taken hold on the future,
　　I see the future
Destructions," he said to the people, he waved his arms,
　　"with a flail
Comes God smiting."
　　　　　　　　　　　　He stood on the hill by the house,
Then Mrs. Morhead looking up from below
Saw him shake his arms over the tops of the buck-eyes
Against the shining cloud and descend rapidly
Behind the trees. She was troubled to think of his
　　passing
Her child by the old corral or beyond the pig-yard,
Yet did not call; she'd been much too indulgent
And little Rachel only came if she pleased.
Meeting the man she felt vaguely he was not alone,
What people were among the trees behind him? Oh,
　　fancies.
"You didn't come in to lunch, you met some people?"
He answered coldly "It would be hard for you
To know what sort of people crying for my help.
As a man swimming dips the free hand forward
Into the wave that has not run by his mouth

I dipped my hand into the future, I was walking
With the people who have not been born yet." She
      thought "He is strange
And good, I cannot understand him, he is very learned."
She said, "You must be very hungry and tired,
I'll have Maruca make you some tea." "Tired, what's
      tired?
There's power." They went toward the house. "How
      old is the house?
Sixty years old?" "My husband's father built it,"
She answered, "it is more than fifty." And Barclay,
      "It is sound, it will stand.
The old man up there?" "My father-in-law. He was
      strong as a redwood,
Everything thrived when he was riding. My husband
Needn't have gone," she said, "they'd never have drafted
      him.
He thought that his father'd manage the place. He was
      proud,"
She said bitterly. "Four months he had been away,
Grandfather's horse rolled over in a gully of bushes,
The old man has been dead from the chest downward.
      He chose
To lie at the top of the house." But Barclay answered,
"The old logs are solid as rock, they'll neither burn nor
      fall down.
This will be standing in the time that I saw
Come up like a red dawn twisted with storms."
She looked sideways with troubled eyes. "The chimney
Had to be propped," she said, "against the south storms.
The brick would stagger, he ran a prop to the roof-
      beam."
He answered: "There is no strong tower that will not
      stagger in that time. I am telling you secrets.

[35]

I've learned something. It's certain that the world has
   changed. The war that your husband returns from
Was only the first blaze in the bark of the tree to mark
   it for the axes." They stood by the stacked fire-
   wood
By the kitchen door, she thinking, "A preacher and has
   read deep books. He's looking at the oakwood."
   Then Barclay: "Not now,
I'll not go in yet. It's hard to hear the rustle and slip
   of the changing stars
Under a roof, I'm going to the sea." Then like a man
   stirring the dark, seeking unconsciously
The word to earthquake her heart: "When you go in,
Kiss Faith Heriot and tell her that what was right is
   wrong, what was wrong's right, the old laws are
   abolished,
They cannot be crossed nor broken, they're dead. The
   sanction is dead. This interval
There is nothing wicked, nothing strange in the world.
   What the heart desires, or any part of the body,
That is the law. The God of the stars has taken his
   hand out of the laws and has dropped them empty
As you draw your hand out of a glove. When I saw
   that he had withdrawn himself out of the churches
I left the church, I was a minister, I told them
God is not here. I came alone into the mountains by
   the sea. Tell your child, tell Faith Heriot.
Tell no one else, these things are secret." The cold
   core of his mind
Smiled at the rest, his mind was split into three parts,
   the cold core
Observing the others, the first in full faith clear-eyed in
   bitter earnestness riding the tides of prophecy,

[36]

The third watching the woman tremble and turn pale,
She had flinched the instant he named Faith Heriot,
  some nerve
Unknown to him was touched, she'd fled up the step to
  the doorway,
Stood pale and framed, her back to the door, between
  the great log-ends
That made the jambs and under the jutting lintel.
"I have knowledge and the world is changed. I have
  power to make you believe.
All that was true when you were a child is rubbed out."
  She wore the gesture
Of a woman standing naked in a door in a dream before
  the hot crowd, and Barclay gently:
"Don't fear. Did I forget to tell you there is nothing
  wicked in the world, no act is a sin?
Nothing you can do is wicked. I have seen God. He
  is there in the hill, he is here in your body.
  My . . . daughter,"
He said shaking, "God thinks through action, I have
  watched him, through the acts of men fighting and
  the acts of women
As much as through the immense courses of the stars;
  all the acts, all the bodies; who dares to enclose
  him
With *this is right* and *that's wrong,* shut his thought
  with scruples, blind him against discoveries, blind
  his eyes?" The brown-skinned
Vaquero, with little Rachel beside, had come down
Across the dooryard hearing the voice lifted;
And the kitchen door opening, Rachel's mother
Drew down from the door-sill, Faith Heriot came out;
  the Indian house-girl,

[37]

Maruca, stood behind her in the door, the broad cheeks
Heavily smiling. Then Barclay, "Have you come to
    hear what I said? It is all secret." Faith Heriot
Caught her friend's hand; "Natalia: what was he saying?
What were you saying that frightened her?" He felt
    Natalia's
Dark eyes like a child's asking pity of his face,
It gave him pleasure, he had power to touch her where
    he pleased, he saw Faith Heriot's
Narrowing blue points of anger; here was the one to
    be humbled, the cut blond hair,
Haggard cheeks, outstretched throat: the cold core of his
    poised mind, without irony, without resentment,
Observed his sexual pleasure in making himself a
    prophet before them, "I am fifty years old!" and
    the competent
Storm of his power: "What was I telling her? You're
    right, it's a bad year for secrets, will yours be
    written,
Yours too over the towers of cities, and shot from hill-
    tops? Yours is so little, Faith Heriot,
But how could I hide mine?" He looked sharply and
    the ax-formed
Young features not changed, not workable metal like
    the others. "Yours will not grow, yours not have
    children," the hard blue
Hardened, "but mine will fly over the world like sun-
    rise. When the world changes and the tired soul
Of the earth drinks a new spring: someone is sent to tell
    men, I am sent to tell you:" he said to the cowboy
"How long since you went to the priest and made con-
    fession?" Who shifted his feet, smiling, shook his
    head, "Long time,"

And Barclay: "You never will need go back to him,
there is no more sin, nothing you could do will need
confession.

Nothing is bad," and turned to Faith Heriot: "All the
relations of the world have changed in a moment.

If there was anything forbidden you may do it. Your
father . . ." he saw the lips twitching and he said

"Your father. Used pleasant sins in his youth . . ."
the lips relaxing,

He said "and now old . . ." "Leave him alone." She
thrust with the throat like a held lance. "Because
you have twisted

This girl with sly talk, scared her with tricks until she
has told you

More than she knows . . ." "I didn't tell him anything
at all," she whispered trembling. "Listened at the
keyhole

The two years back then. What is it, a sneaking evan-
gelist?" It stood so clearly in Barclay's mind what
to answer,

Though it had no reason in his mind, he answered: "I
know that what you told her was lies." He thought
of the woman

By the well-curb in Samaria, convert for having been
told her own story. "I have more power than I
know."

But willing to use it further he doubted it, he feared
the words would come wrong, be merely ridiculous;
he had touched

Something: and the torrent would serve: "Did you think
who had seen into the mind of God had not into
yours?

The hill is gray with dead grass and the ocean

[39]

Blazing violet and blue, but a girl is clean white under
　　the clothes, white as milk, but under
The white skin, under the dead grass, in the blue crystal:
Red blood, white stone, black water: God is there also:
The same who is like a river swirling the stars like
　　straws: I am telling you the river
Turns sharp around the rock of this year.　He gave a
　　man laws on a mountain, your old commandments,
Cut them in stone: I tell you that every letter of the
　　laws is struck backward, the stone tables turned
　　over,
The stars are flowing another way and the people
Shall learn a new flight.　I was a preacher in a church
　　in the city: I knew all the while
That God was not an old man in the sky saying like an
　　old man
Be good, my children: I knew that he was fiercer than
　　a lion in the night and lovelier than a girl
Alone and naked on the shore in the sea's breath, nearly
　　too young to be loved, yellow-haired: and I looked,
He let go the bent bough, he lifted his feet from the
　　flattened grass, made all the laws nothing.　What
　　purpose?
He will have confusion for its beauty, he is wild to
　　walk in new ways, he snatches at the rose of burn-
　　ing,
He stirs in the earth: Is a little freedom not worth
　　destruction?"　He stopped, the five were silent, and
　　he said
"Nothing is asked, what could be wanted?　The whole
　　earth will hear it."

VI

He rounded the house toward the road seaward.
They saw him between the low oak-bush and the log wall
Moving his arms as if a multitude waited
Outside the gap-roofed sheds.   When he was gone they
    were silent,
When he returned in the evening he also was silent.
He slept badly, he heard in the night the young child
Crying, he had thought that Rachel's mother Natalia
Slept in the same room, but the child cried
Uncomforted.

                Came the thought "I am sterile as a bone
In lack of action: God thinks through action: akh, talk!
Talk and thoughts, though I felt a power straining
    within me.
And then I am emptied and lie in a bed like a pit
And have achieved nothing, all that I said
Was folly and there is no deliverance."   He thought
"The act is deliverance.   What act? . . . What are they
    doing
Lets the child cry and cry in the night?
I preached freedom and found none.   Deliverance.   De-
    liverance,"
He sighed and slept.   He awoke thinking of April
His daughter, her purity and grace, named from the
    springtime,

[41]

And running his hand through the stiff growth on his
    chin
He thought "I am loathsome. God is in every creature,
In toads and curded excrement." He thought of Maruca,
The strong brown servant who fed the table: like a
    toad's
Her thick body and broad face . . . "Oh! Back in
    adolescence?"
He cried to himself, a vision of the thick brown body
Rising against him like a giantess: no gesture,
Only the form, female as moist brown earth,
The heavy protuberances of breast and belly
And the idol thighs. Light had come, certainly she
    stirred
And was born from the stale bed. "Death is horrible,"
    he thought,
"Rot in brown soil." He stretched himself stiffly in the
    bed,
Entered death, little arrows shook in his brain and were
    silent.
The years one by one, green in front, brown behind,
Passed and dropped grass-mold over. "Not dead, not
    yet,"
He cried to himself under the earth and thrust up
The burden for breath. That suffocation
Conquered him when he looked at Maruca, he came to
    her
After three days; she had fed the henyard and gone up
Among the twisted buck-eyes, he breathing with anguish,
The nightmare band around his chest: "I have money.
Dollars. I have come to buy deliverance. Listen
    Maruca,
I am Lazarus, I am Lazarus up from the dead,
Chastity has withered my bones, there is nothing I want

Less than you. How old are you, twenty?" She smiled
    under the stolid cheek-bones,
Shook her head, the Asian-lidded eyes had no change.
He sobbing for breath: "How can I live unless you will
    do it?
It is not that I want anything, never, never want,
Clear-eyed as to that, not die blind as to that,
It is all," he said swaying drunkenly, "a matter of de-
    liverance."
He fumbled in his purse. "Here are ten dollars . . .
    four dollars.
Take them. You know that you are much stronger than
    I am,
How could you be afraid of me?" She clutched and
    nodded,
"To-night." "Oh," he cried gasping, "not in the house.
Oh!" and the hand shuddered to the face, "there is some
Reason against the . . . house. They walk all night
    there,
That's not the reason. The passions die in old age
But I have shot back to puberty." He said, "It's a
    symbol,
Mode of deliverance." His hand, cold but quite dry,
Fastened on the warm brown wrist. She hung back,
    firm-planted,
Immovable. He said, "I have more money I will give
    you,"
And drawing her along behind the twisted buck-eyes,
"You heard me that sin's abolished, it's not for that
    freedom.
As for desire, there's nothing in the world Maruca
I desire less than you. Crack the diamond breast-plate,
Chastity that sucks the power of prophets." They left
    the buck-eyes,

And over a ridge of crumbled earth and dead grass
To a dry stream-bed stubbed with dwarf oaks. She
     halting
In the yellow pit that winter cataracts had sunk,
Hard green dry leaves shielded, "Now must go back
To work. Much work." He said, "Here is too open.
Up farther. You want more money." He thought, "She
     will follow,"
And broke up through the boughs to the next level,
"Must I kiss? Agh." He reached her hand, drew her
     up,
The anguish it was to draw breath had ceased and a
     flare
Lit in his brain. She seemed not to resent;
To invite. "I am of the higher race and perhaps
For that reason not horrible to her. If an angel
Came old, shaking and mad to someone of mine,"
He thought under the steady internal lightning,
"How my hand shakes." Though he was focussed on
     the act of deliverance,
Disinterested voices in his brain all the while
Like insects back of a searchlight: "It is fifteen years.
I was thirty-five." The mass, hard thickness of her body
Astonished him. "To master the people, set myself
     free
To master the people. Pleasure would be contemptible."
The light waned, he despaired; suddenly a twitching
Vision of finer limbs, and he thought that the dead
Are dead forever, the inexorable seal across them.
The enduring animal, the God. To live, in itself's
A triumph. The light had grown vast, now suddenly
     and softly
It was extinguished. Kneeling to rise, he thought,
     "There is certainly

One power, and all its forms are equal before it.
I call it God to the people." The woman was asking
    him
To keep a promise about money and he doubled
What he had meant to give her. He was careless and
    freed.
She had to be reminded that it made eight dollars.
When she was gone: "I have bought salvation!" He
    broke
Another exit under the thicket branches.
Crossing the hill in the swirl and storm of sunlight,
Where were they? the invisible multitude he had felt
    following
Wherever he went? "They were a sign, now they peel
    off me
Against the instant fulfilment."

                              He saw from far up . . .
Maruca? in the form of his daughter? He peered under
    his hand against the wild sun. It gave him great
    happiness
To feel the visions kindle in his brain, the confusion of
    persons. "There is no distinction, each individual
The one power fills and forms, bubbles of one breath.
    I lay in a woman's lap uniting myself
With the infinite God." Maruca? She wrung her
    hands, didn't she, turning and returning,
The vined porch and the road: the Indian woman would
    never
That side the house: gazed toward the sea and then
    gazed
Toward the hills. April. Why there was the car. He
    went down
Brushing the dusty and stained cloth with his hands,
He wore no hat, smoothing his hair and trembling.

VII

"Father." (I knew her when she was a baby, I fed her
 milk from the bottle.)
"You've come to see me?" Straining to adjust his mind
To new experience, and the actual reality her presence:
Wears blue, cut short: nearly as blond as Faith Heriot:
 the infinite between them,
The infinite distance. She's tired. "Yes," she answered,
 "you wouldn't come.
Mother's in the cottage at Point Pinos. I'll never ask
 you
Your reason, you've a good reason." "I have left
 reasons behind . . ."
                                    "Oh," she answered,
"She's been sick, sick. Her suffering. When I tell you,
Then you'll come home." "I have come home out of
 death, I am Lazarus, an hour ago, April,
I entered the dead." He trembled with exultance, he
 was telling her everything, her maidenhood, "went
 down to the dead
And mixed myself with the dead race. I am out of the
 maps,
Breaking strange waves." "Death," she answered bit-
 terly, "is what
I have had to listen to her crying for. Come sit in the
 car,

That woman is watching us from the rose-vines." He
    sat beside her,
He fancied she edged away from him. "It will look
    better when it's grown,"
He said, touching his chin, "I had no razor.
There's not a gray hair." Vaguely in his mind it sym-
    bolized
The new growth of his life from the sharp break.
The head was gray, the old life was over, the brown
    beard
Like a new thundering of youth. But April: "The news-
    papers
Tormented her, she was ashamed to see friends, she
    couldn't live in the city.
Have you seen the papers?" "Why, no. It would
    make no difference.
You cannot understand, April, how utterly
The hive's hum's hushed. Papers." "She had nothing,"
    she answered.
"You, I don't know what you have, some vision, some
    thunder
That drowns the noises. I'm not a Christian . . ."
    "I'm glad
My teaching," he said, "when I was a fool was fruitless.
No infection." "But mother had you and Christ. Ed-
    ward was dead.
You took both in one day. Oh, she still tries
To imagine that her religion's a rock
And you appointed to punishment or repentance.
But the time has struck in. It's all shadows. You can
    see, father,
She's like someone falling and snatching at the air.
Religion? She'd bought poison, I stole it from her
And hid it here under the seat of the car. I hardly

[47]

Dared leave her to-day." He moved his hand sidewise,
Palm downward, like one erasing a scripture. "Not lie,
To myself nor you." "Ah, we're not friends then," she
answered,
Trembling. "Lives aren't split off so easily. If I must
choose . . ."
"There's no distinction, choice is fantastic," he answered,
"No distinction of persons." April was silent
A little, and cold-eyed: "It doesn't much matter
That all you say's like a night fog where a torch
Sometimes passes but nobody sees the torch-bearer.
I came to ask you to come home, I only ask you
To go and see her and return. But now I must go up,
It will be night-time." "I'll give you something,"
He said "for Audis, your mother. Tell her that the laws
Are abolished, let her cast out scruples like devils,
Tear down the walls, run naked, she has starved all her
life.
And tell her to act, God thinks through action. You too
April:
The act is deliverance: Oh it is more besides; discovery;
I know, for I drank it
When you were on the road and while you came to the
door: it has changed me
From a cold stone to a star: all the relations of the
world have been changed in a moment, mine to her,
Yours to me April. Before, when I said freedom, I
stammered." He descended from the car. "My
people,"
He said, "must hear what I say." Though his voice was
not raised
It made her shudder, his confidence of a multitude
Under the snake-limbed oaks leaning up canyon,
By the ruinous barns in the light of the bronze hills

Sun-beaten from seaward: though there was no one she
  also
Felt the spectral disciples gathered; and he said, "I held
  you in my arms,
There is no distinction of persons. . . . You were a
  baby, I held you in my arms, I fed you milk from
  the bottle,
God that grows up in trees and mountains, the same
  power
In the wrinkled limbs formed them and smoothed them,
  drew them long, polished them white and shining,
  mounded the low breasts,
Made beautiful the throat: he made you slender who
  made the servant Maruca like a pine block: the
  same power,
There is no distinction of persons, it is flame in all
  lamps: and blew a bone bubble on the head of the
  column
To hold his glory: yours he made beautiful with light
  brown
Hair, hers with dull black: I have light and fire to fill it
  with shining, as if the sun were shut up
In the little bone sky. . . . But you April, I will tell
  you quietly,
You think me insane because I have learned something:
Does the mad father April not need your caring
As much as the bitter mother? Bring her to this hill,
I have what will heal it. I am not insane, I'd be con-
  tent to be,
To have learned causes and sources and have had the
  lightning
Lighten my thirst. I have many streams running in the
  mind,
They mingle on the lips, no matter, each one flows pure,

And purest of all the one that I dare not think of.
But as for the people that I named: when you looked
    sideways
To see what multitude my madness invented
Under the oaks, by the ruinous barns, in the bronze hills:
Indeed there are minds knitted with mine, I have never
    met them,
When I send out my thought there are nerves to take it,
Yes, in these hills, and in that city: and they will come
    down,
They need not: they hear."

VIII

At the supper-table he asked Natalia
Whether she could make room for his wife and daughter,
"They are coming in a few days." "My husband's
  coming,"
She said, "next month. Almost a year they've kept
  him
Since the war came to an end." She looked at Faith
  Heriot,
Who, suddenly rising and her face like the plaster
That striped the house outside between the black logs,
"Why shouldn't they come? Oh you'll be glad of com-
  pany.
The girl who was here, that's his daughter, that came in
  the car,
Perhaps can earn her way keeping the old bones
Under the roof when I have gone out of this place.
She'll never take them out riding." Natalia: "Ah,
  Faith.
Are you so tired?" "Why should I wait for next
  month?"
She answered. Natalia half rose to follow her, then
  mournfully:
"Oh, there's still room in the house. Till Randal comes
  home."
They heard Faith Heriot move upstairs like a restless
Fire in the hallway. "Before you take out the plates,
Maruca, fix a tray for my father." Then angrily

Regarding the two farmhands, the Spanish one and the
    other,
At the end of the table, "When my husband comes home
Things will get done on the place," she said to Barclay,
"The stock be saved, we shan't need to keep boarders.
The fields be plowed and planted, the horses not die."
She took the tray and went out to the stairway. Maruca
Gathering the plates leaned over Barclay's chair
So that the great breast, through the oily brown cloth,
Lay on his shoulder, he overlooked his repugnance,
Unmoved, secretly smiling: the symbolic flesh
Had served him: the value of the symbol secured,
By-product amorousness, the ridiculous female
After-glow had no finger on; "I have cast the last fear:
Of being ridiculous."

               Later, he had walked in the twilight
Of the slight moon, he had peace and confidence, the
    sharp-tipped crescent
Reddened and fell in the sea beyond the Sur rock.
    Barclay returning
Felt someone meet him in the dark porch under the
    rose-vines, and a hand touching him, he thought
    Maruca's,
He pushed it down, saying readily, "What do you want?
    I have no love in me."

               Not the Indian's voice, though a whisper:
"You know something: tell me what I must do: come
    outside.
I've waited for you." She turned sharp to the left,
Too furtive to take the path, staying under the wall
Until they reached the windowless corner and had come
By the oak-bush; the face under the sky-gleam Natalia's,
But lamplike whitened and changed: "You are good:
    and I know

Your eyes can measure the hidden bones of one's trouble.
Nothing looks wicked to you, nothing looks loathsome,
I know you saw it."
               That she had had a child was no matter.
The intoxicant, slender body by him in the star-gleam,
Appealing to him, ready to make herself bare with con-
    fession:
That was one stream in the mind; it was most marvellous,
And not quite sanity, that he could see his own mind
Objectively, all the currents and courses at one moment:
That one, the sexual pleasure: this other, his authority
Acknowledged; he'd not been confident before: here, for
    this hunting,
Disciples, this one the first, lances to ambush
The power behind powers, bring down the mastodon:
    one current
Opaque yet, he understood it vortexed on April:
"And this when I have the time and have dared examine
    it,
The earth will be crystal:" he answered Natalia, "I
    told you,
God, turning like a quick seal under the water,
Swims the other current: or like a snake has rubbed off
Old customs, the courts and churches sell the dry skin
Sloughed from the fire of his coils: there is nothing
    wicked,
No sin, no wrong, no possible fountain of shame:
And the earth shines with aliveness: how could you be
    troubled?"
She trembled and said, "The man that I love is com-
    ing."
"Are you not glad?"   "I thought you had knowledge.
    Oh, no matter.
I'm glad," she said, turning.   He felt his authority

Slip in the dark like a rope slipping, and angrily:
"If it was only to say that you have more loves than
    that one: you needn't
Have crossed my evening of thought. Two are not too
    many, the man and his child, will three
Break down the basket? You are not a virgin to see the
    world through rainbows." She closed her eyes and
    he saw
The muscles of the face quiver. "Through nightmares."
    The mouth grinned like a mask. "I have kept her
    off for five days,"
She muttered against the teeth, "but I am afraid.
I took her in, she was sick and helpless, she had no-
    where to go." He answered, "You may do any-
    thing.
If you have pleasure in being under two masters:
Choice is a fool. Why have you denied her?" She
    turned
Silently back toward the house. Then Barclay, "It is I
That am your master and I tell you play with your
    playmates.
Fear nothing, for I will gather them also. I have
    strength.
And God is kindly, you may couple in his hands.
But if you fear the anger of lovers: only starved minds
Child the idiot jealousy: I have come to feed them."
    She went
Like one who in a famine has been given strange bread
And takes it home, hiding it under his coat,
Doubtful whether it is death or life that he carries
Hungering, and will lock the doors and perhaps
Not dare to be fed.

IX

Faith Heriot ranged the house like a fire.
In the afternoon Barclay, as his manner was, wandered
Up the hill to a certain rock, starved ledge of limestone
Breaking the slope above an abandoned cabin.
From here the great shed of the mountain shot in bronze
  folds,
Seemed humming like bells under the strokes of the
  sun; in the creases the winter stream-beds,
Haired with low oak, but higher between deep ridges
  spiring to redwood, netted the edge of the continent
With many-branching black threads; the wall steepened
  below and went down
To a sea like blue steel breakless to Asia, except the
  triangle-shaped sand-flat as low as the ocean.
The lighthouse rock apexed, and the lesser morro
Flanked on the south; these two alone breaking the
  level
Opposite the straight sea-wall of the ended world.

Barclay was silent although his people
Expected words. He knew that this multitude
Was in a manner unreal . . . certainly the human
Earth knew its leader though not yet consciously; the
  deep
Layers of the islanded points of mind that are peaks
Risen from one base, thronged him from far, whose
  fatal

Perceptions and discoveries were making the future.
The future thronged him, the inevitable unborn
Inhabitants of this mountain, him making their lives—
He did not think expressly, it lay at the thought's root—
More than that Meccan camel-driver had made
The lands keyed on Arabia . . . he too was grown old
When revelation rained from the desert stars;
He too fled from his city and founded a church
On alien earth. . . . Were inhuman presences
Mixed in this people, beasts running, rocks moving,
Horned heads, heads of dark leaves? He stood up on
    the rock,
And quietly, hardly speaking aloud; but they all could
    hear him:
"What have I hidden, why do you still hang on my
    mind, will you have the perceptions
Embryo? My giants will all arise from their fountain
When time ripens. There are those among you that
    neither breathe nor feed, limestone fire-hardened,
    old lava,
Granite with the wet sea's growth; others that breathe
    through leaves and through roots
Milk the earth; those able to wait millenniums and these
    many green centuries: I am speaking to the one
    consciousness,
Modulated through wood and through stone, through
    the nerves of man, the flesh of cattle: you that
    wear horns
And suffer in this drought, but few seasons to live: that
    which suffers, I tell you,
Is not another thing from the disdain of the stones, not
    another
From the bull's joy dipping the blood-red whip-stock

In the honey of the womb: if this one thing enjoys and
   suffers, equally, equally at length, and in cool
Reclusion in the stone is utterly itself,
Then its existence, not its color in each form in each
   moment, not pain nor pleasure
That cancel each other . . ." He saw the horned fore-
   heads
Turn down hill to watch someone approaching
His people from the low oaks, a woman, and he said:
"Though one had eighty years of delight and another
From birth to old age pain, pain: the one is the other,
   the delight
And pain are cancelled the one existence approving
   them,
The one consciousness: the one breath of the organ
   blown through innumerable
Conduits of sound; blessed are the ears that hear eternal
   music." She approached and he said, "Maruca,
I am speaking to those you cannot see: but stand among
   them."
She looked at the cattle thinking, "They are steers and
   lean cows,
And now they are winding away over the hillside."
She stood before the limestone, smiling her lure, and
   Barclay:
"Nothing is ridiculous. Laughter and sentimentality
Are poured from the one pitcher, the pure in their
   minds
Taste all things, not those." She answered, "Nobody
   saw me
Come up from the house, much work, soon must go back.
I thought it's not good for him to be alone
And talk to yourself. Nobody ever

Comes to the small dead house down here: soon must
    go back."
"There is nothing ridiculous: but I have emptied your
    cup,"
He answered; she approaching he said, "Stand there!"
    and he said:
"What I did with this flesh is no importance:
Except I was lamed with a chain, the act filed it. But
    look at her,
Earth, and you trees that covered us, you lichen-sided
Boulders of the shore: you chiefly, air-wandering or
    time-traversing presences of men,
Drift of the coast and drifted down from the future to
    hear me, worship her a little, it is this that saves
    you.
Self-regardful humanity cutting itself away from the
    earth and the creatures, gathered home on itself,
Digging a pit behind it and a gulf before it,
Cancerous, a growth that makes itself alien: how long
    would you be spared before the knife rings you
    and the spreading
Ulcer scooped out, but this sound flesh solders you home
    to the beasts? It is human yet of dark mind,
And never has cut the navel-string and draws from the
    mother, pleads between you and destruction: this,
    here, your Savior:
Worship it a while.
                I am not your savior, I have
    sharper gifts than salvation."
                The Indian perplexed and vacant
Looked sidelong, compelled in the net of imagination,
    darkly
Feeling multitude behind her, then clearly hearing

Motion on the hill: and Barclay across the steam of his
    people
Like a low ground-fog breaking to horns and branches
In the blinding sun, perceived two others; and the one:
"He preaches and your fat Maruca's the church,
That's why she slid away so quietly up hill."
He said, "It is bitter herbs, Faith Heriot, God chooses.
The earth is full of sweet leaves: you for your bitter-
    ness.
I am speaking to those you cannot see: stand there
    among them."

X

The fog-bank that all day far off had lain slant
On the sea northward, perhaps indeed had drawn in-
   land
And covered the shore like a flood and climbed up the
   hill-slope.
Though the sun blazed there came a ground-fog; and the
   wind
Was like the draught from a cellar, from the low sea
Sharp with its odors.
                              It was not the low fog.
The man had something in him, confidence, power . . .
   power? . . .
Enforced his own hallucination on his witnesses.
Then had he called, others to come up? For he was
   saying
"I believe faithfully that I was sent to you. What else
   then
Woke in me alone, me alone
The edged confidence, the perfect desire, one-eyed,
   thousand-handed,
To conquer knowledge like a capital city taken in one
   storm,
One dawn, then all the provinces are flat? Others have
   trenched the suburbs and never an end: lance the
   heart:
Power is one power:" while he was saying; and the
   three

Apart from each other, Natalia, Faith Heriot, the Indian,
Stared up through the incomprehensible torrent of prophecy
At him crowned with gray hair and sunlight, two horsemen
Rode through the fog up the hill; they halted a little
At the spectral edge of his hallucination, the spurs
Clinked when they slid to the earth.

       "Not for salvation,"
He said, "for perfection. I bring fire and not salt.
The time leaps at its end." If the half understood
Words alone enforced the vision, then one of his hearers
Would have seen in her mind a cat spring at its prey but another a sea-wave
Shot at the rock: they all with one soul
Saw a naked child leap into fire; so clearly Natalia
Cried out thinking of her child; but one of the newcomers:
"I saw it yesterday!" And Barclay, "What did you see
Yesterday?" "The blinded child." He answered, "But the eyes
Ate the white heart before they blackened." Then the other horseman
(One saw his face flicker in the multitude, Joe Medina,
The dark one of the two vaqueroes at Morhead's)
Said, "This my friend Vasquez, Onorio Vasquez
Who sees visions." Vasquez: "I live north
On Palo Corona mountain, I saw God at Point Sur
Flaming about this time yesterday." Then Barclay,
Looking at Maruca, "It was immaculate of pleasure.
What form had the God?" "Master," he answered, "a flaming child.

But who are all these that hear you, thousands on the
    hillside?"
First after him for Natalia the fog
Organized into faces beyond faces, the doubled illusion
Enforcing itself against her; then the vaquero
Medina saw the heads and shoulders like waves of a sea
Break the plain gray; Maruca at that moment equally;
    Faith Heriot
Cried to herself, "I am all alone, there is no one
On the hill," and angrily closed her eyes but had seen
Not human heads, hawks' heads and horned heads and
    sharp wings,
Stones and the peaks of redwoods.
                      Where yesterday
Only one visionary from Palo Corona mountain
Felt Barclay's mind, to-day these five reverberating
The vision enforced and focussed it, so that whoever on
    the coast from the Carmel southward
Was vacant of desire a moment: one of the Victorines at
    Mal Paso, Woodfinn at Garapatas,
Myrtle Cartwright, Vogler's daughter up the Big Sur,
    Gonzalez on the hill far southward, Higuera
Under Pico Blanco: each without knowing a reason
    turned the eyes toward Point Sur: so that when
    word came
Of a man wielding powers and prophecies, they were not
    incredulous, they seemed to have known it before.
    But old Morhead,
The paralyzed old man under the farmhouse roof,
    imagined that lightning
Lay on the roof or fire was free in the house: he had no
    one by him,
And cried aloud in hollow loneliness.

Then Barclay:

"They are gathered to me. God is become a child:
    scimitar of light
On the dark rim in the evening. Not the power but the
    soul
Crescents or wanes between the nights of the centuries.
Can a child sin? What's done is that child doing it,
    and what has been done?
War, torture, famine; oppressions; the secret cruelties;
    the plague in the air that killed its millions; that
    child
Reaping a fly's wings, innocently laughing
From the rich heart? Oh it has no laughter though a
    child. It is tortured with its own earnestness, it is
    tortured.
It is lonely: what playmate? It has no mother.
The child that is the stars and the earth and men's
    bodies, and the hollow darkness
Outside the stars, and the dark hollow in the atom."
    (He thought, "What do I know? I speak of my-
    self.
Am I that child?) Hollow and hollow and dark, is there
    any substance?
                    There's power. What does it
    want, power?
It tortures its own flesh to discover itself. Of humanity
What does it want? It desires monsters. I told you it
    had changed.
Once it commanded justice, charity, self-continence,
Love between persons, loyalty: it was wise then: what
    purpose?
To hold the pack together for its conquest of the earth.
Now the earth is conquered, there is room, you have
    built your mountain, there is no competitor,

It says *Flame!* it has sent me with fire, did you dream
That those were final virtues? your goodness, your
    righteousness,
Your love: rags for the fire."
                       He groaned in his heart,
Feeling himself like a shell hollowed, the weakness,
The diminution, the awful voice not his own
Blown through his void.
                  "I have come to establish you
Over the last deception, to make men like God
Beyond good and evil. There is no will but discovery,
No love but toward that tragic child, toward the mother-
    less,
The unlaughing, the lonely."
                    The fog had climbed
    higher and his head
Was hidden, only they heard his voice falling from above
    them
Until it had ceased.

XI

Each one had stood lonely in a multitude.
Each felt about him the stir of multitude disparting,
The fog whitening in currents. They called to each
other
Softly and afraid. When Joe Medina came out to the
horses
One stood yet, Onorio's was gone. When he saw some-
one
Drift by him, it was Maruca, afraid of the steers.
She told him she had much work at the house but he
answered
No one need work now, he left the horse tethered
And led her by the arm.

                Over the mound of the slope
Faith Heriot found Natalia sobbing. She heard the
fog-horn
Blow hoarse minutes from the lighthouse on the rock
of Point Sur.
Her father whom she had left was the lighthouse-keeper,
She tenderly and fiercely: "Natalia, you hear him call
me?
If you put me by, I will go back." Who, sobbing: "I
love you."
"But now," she answered, "you've had a letter from
Randal
And see eyes in the door." "He's coming, when he
comes

What shall I do?" She trembled hearing far down
The hoarse throat from the rock. Faith Heriot stood
    rigid,
Her narrow face under the wet yellow hair
The fog's color, and said slowly "I am still good enough
To nurse the old dead man. Randal," she said against
    the set teeth,
"Will not be at home always. Not days. The nights,"
She muttered shaking all rigid in the curded white
From the ground, like a stone pillar when the earth
    is shaken,
"Are your business;" the blue eyes ringed with dim white
Seemed shelterless of lids or lashes and the lips
Strained in a smile, "I have looked forward for a long
    time
To the midnights with hell opened under the floor.
I will be quiet." And Natalia: "Oh yes. Oh yes, yes.
Is that man crazy? What did he mean? Did we see
    people?"
"He means we must live as long and merrily as pos-
    sible."

Barclay climbed upward the slope. High up the gray
    fog
Was split in tongues, and over the bald summit blue sky.
    A man approached him
And said, "You've got outside humanity: you will not
    return.
Oh, let them feed and clothe you, you have money:
    but neither in love nor instruction
Lean to that breed." "Love?" he said, "what is love?"
    But the other: "To what purpose
Have you been dropping wine and fire in the little
    vessels?" When the buried sun

Rosed an arched banner of the mist, then Barclay saw
the lean face, the stub of brown beard, the bar of
the eyebrows,
His own mirrored; and the image: "If you did not love
them would you labor to lead them?" He shaking
and smiling:
"I see the devil is short of faces." It answered, "You
could not fool yourself utterly. Your very body
Cries for companions; you stood like a moose bellowing
for love. I listened all the while with secret
laughter
The time we persuaded ourself we wanted disciples to
bait the God-trap: their sweet persons you wanted;
Their eyes on our eyes. A filthy breed to refer to."
And Barclay, "Here you are, madness.
The Magus Zoroaster thy dead . . . Where else does
consciousness
Burn up to a point but in the bone lamps? I should be
lonely." It laughed, "As the tragic child?" "He
includes them.
And I though I choke, old portrait . . ."

                                    In the ruinous cabin
Down the slope under the limestone ridge and the
darkening fog
Medina said in his language, "If you'd go naked
And the face covered you'd have dozens of lovers.
Needs a strong man like me not to be frightened
By the face . . ." Maruca clinging and resisting: "Oh,
oh,
Let me alone." She clawed his cheek, then he dizzily
Feeling astonished with a splendor of happiness
Twisted her arm saying, "Now will you let me? Now
will you?

Will you? Now will you Maruca?" "Ao! Ay! Que
si."

Barclay on the dome of the hill: "Old counterfeit,
Eye-thing, the hand would go through. Before I annul
you
With one finger's experience: tell me what's the magic
in bipeds? I see the stone and the tree
Through sheet crystal." "Ah, that's our private im-
purity: but look at the majesty of things, a race of
atomies
Obsess you? Except them till the stars are counted,
The bad crumb will digest, the apes that walk like
herons
Nook themselves in." But Barclay looked at the sky,
the long tassels of the fog reddening recurved;
At the earth, the bits of quartz in the stubble; and a
shiver of laughter
Twitched in his nerves. "Oh that's," he said twitching,
"confession. Single-hearted is clean of laughter:
What is it that I dare not think of?" He thought Faith
Heriot had moods of feature like April's . . .
"Why," the image answered,
"Of your own mind hypnotized by the accidents of birth
and begetting. Because you have coupled and are
budded
Of couplers: humanity the only pillar on every horizon?"
                    Deep under the darkening fog-sea
Natalia turned suddenly on her companion: "I am not
ashamed
And if there were crowds: are there crowds on the hill-
side?

I'd do it in front of the cowboys, I'm full of cowardice,
The shining sacrifice." Faith Heriot regarded her with
wonder
Through the gray plumes: "Long ago, when you were
kind,
I used to lie awake in bed, the old log
Groaning past midnight, and dream wide awake
There were men tied to trees and you Natalia
All undressed in front of them and ashamed and afraid,
I saw their clothes humped with the hateful pillars,
When I came in, bare too, and we showed them . . .
Oh,
The beasts not needed, the shining sacrifice . . .
They'd scream with desire, I'd say to you, 'The trees are
screaming,'
I'd strike them with my fists and return to you. I never
told you."
"Dear," she answered trembling, "is the fog full of faces
around us?"
"No," she answered. "Oh but I think it is full of
watchers,
Dear hands, oh dear hands." The moving circle of
starved sod
They trod in the dome of the fog suddenly was chorded
With a dark brink and a deep pit of drawn vapor.
They entered the dry stream-bed like entering a cavern
And wrestled together under the stub of dwarf oaks
With hoarse gaspings and little cries. Natalia
Imagined with fearful joy on both the clay banks
Watchers; but Faith Heriot was like a falcon
Wild with famine.
                    The mirror-image on the hill in
        the sundown: "Out of love destruction.

There was not one word but savored of sudden burning:
   but all for love's sake." And Barclay, "Have it
   then, I love them."
"And feed the loved poison? You knew they were not
   stone but paper fagots to the fire of your saying.
Love that destroys?" Barclay looked right and left
   like an animal
Driven on a trap, the funnel of the high stockade nar-
   rowing. He muttered quickly, lowering his head:
"If they were finished: peace, peace. I have both the
   desires. May not one hate
The loved, love the hated, where does this fountain
   from?" When he looked
The inquisitor was dim; only the face, and that fading,
   hung opposite his eyes
On no stalk, and dissolved. There was a dizzy fugitive
   sickness at heart and the whirling had stopped,
So that he said gathering his functions to life, "Love
   requires martyrs: seal it with martyrdom:" he re-
   membered
That both his father and his son were dead. "Love of
   humanity: the enormous picture of familiar passions.
I have conquered the tempter: who came in the image
   of the most hated: I am conquering the loved."

Onorio Vasquez rode out to a promontory:
The little seer of visions who never sees anything
But tangent to things: never worth seeing: and his pony
On the point of the hill, distrusting both declivities in
   the blind fog,
Stood; then the rider turned in the saddle and the hill
Was lit with arches: on the left a tender steep fog-bow
Footed about that desert cabin they had passed,
Pale-shining arc of a parabola drew upward;

On the right the like radiance, the equal steep fog-bow
Footed high up the gully that severed the hillside.
But where they crossed at the top was a shining trouble
In the strained fog as if a star had come down
To rest on the forked arcs; and the evening darkening
Onorio peered into the scars on his palms
And said, "He is darker to himself than to men.
He is neither a child nor a man, he has no understanding.
He is terrible," he said with tranquil eyes.
He intended the multiform God but it was Barclay on
    the hilltop.
Who feeling again his multitude gathered in the spectral
    glimmer: "Fear nothing: I have conquered: not a
    hair of your heads
Falls to the fire. Oh little ones, passionate maiden
    bodies and April faces if I had proved enemy
What power in the huge world . . ." He widened his
    arms opposite the flaring sun-fall. "I have chosen
    you for love."

XII

Here were new idols again to praise him;
I made them alive; but when they looked up at the
    face before they had seen it they were drunken and
    fell down.
I have seen and not fallen, I am stronger than the idols,
But my tongue is stone how could I speak him? My
    blood in my veins is seawater how could it catch
    fire?
The rock shining dark rays and the rounded
Crystal the ocean his beam of blackness and silence
Edged with azure, bordered with voices;
The moon her brittle tranquillity; the great phantoms,
    the fountains of light, the seed of the sky,
Their plaintive splendors whistling to each other:
There is nothing but shines though it shine darkness;
    nothing but answers; they are caught in the net of
    their voices
Though the voices be silence; they are woven in the
    nerve-warp.
One people, the stars and the people, one structure;
    the voids between stars, the voids between atoms,
    and the vacancy
In the atom in the rings of the spinning demons,
Are full of that weaving; one emptiness, one presence:
    who had watched all his splendor
Had known but a little: all his night, but a little.

I made glass puppets to speak of him, they splintered
in my hand and have cut me, they are heavy with
my blood.
But the jewel-eyed herons have never beheld him
Nor heard; nor the tall owl with cat's ears, the bittern
in the willows, the squid in the rock in the silence
of the ocean,
The vulture that broods in the pitch of the blue
And sees the earth globed, her edges dripping into rain-
bow twilights: eyed hungers, blind fragments: I
sometime
Shall fashion images great enough to face him
A moment and speak while they die. These here have
gone mad: but stammer the tragedy you crackled
vessels,

XIII

April had promised that if her mother wanted
They'd return the next day, but Audis Barclay
Each time they dropped south from a ridge felt gates
Close on the road; on the highest last hilltop
They left the road and dropped westward; then it was
      determined,
She thought, that having yielded and come barred the
      exit;
And all the road not a hill nor a tree remembered,
Lost in exhausting sleep. This was his lair:
Bronze hills, gray oaks. Then high over wrecked farm-
      sheds
The prison of black logs striped with white plaster, the
      flaring
Sea-fog of autumn sundown. They came to the porch
Rotting under its rose-vine, all the leaves fallen.
Barclay opened the door, someone behind him,
And said quietly, "I knew it was you. Are you tired?
I have gained strange experience and felt you on the
      way.
Two hours ago I told you Natalia. Natalia Morhead.
My daughter April. My wife." Audis her slender cold
      hand touched Barclay's: "Are you well, Arthur?"
      Though indeed
It was touching a strange man's. April with her eyes
Assumed superiority over Natalia;

And Barclay: "At Sovranes Canyon the road
Cuts between hills, I saw you there in the car,
And like iron gates behind you on the hills for pillars
Closing behind you." Audis whitened and answered,
"I remember nothing of the road, were there gates
      April?"
"No, mother." And Barclay: "I draw the region
      through my mind;
I have other streams in my mind." She felt herself
      taken
His prisoner; and pale, cold, silent, bitterly crying
To herself, "Oh that I'd never come," she appeared
To the others in the house his prisoner. At the supper
      table
She murmured that she was too tired to eat, and April
Followed her up the stairs. Her things had been carried
To Barclay's room, April's to the room beside it.
"I must sleep with you April, I have no other place."
She undressed and knelt by the bed, April regarded her
With curious pity. She prayed formally aloud,
And after she had lain down the lips kept moving
Without sound. April blew out the lamp,
Went slowly down to her father. "I think we'll go back
To-morrow morning, first I must talk to you. I brought
Mother: what will you do?" He was pacing the floor
In the big room, the door was open to the other,
He stopped and said loudly, "Did that cost blood?
Brought her? I am making the world, I hold the in-
      tolerable weight
In my hands while I make it, I bear the strain, strain."
      She bitterly:
"I ought to have known. But is it needful
To tell the whole house how much we have to be sorry
      for?"

She thought anxiously "Oh, where?" and said "Let us
go
And walk in the road, you walk in the night you told
me
Often." He said, "Decision?" and softly, "decision?
We'll talk on the road," he said quietly, she followed
him
And saw the slit of a moon move in the leafless rose-vine
To die in a pearled cloud. He turned and walked fast
Down the hill, she thought "He wants to get by the
farm-sheds."
She felt dwindled to early childhood, the strides
Rapid and long to follow, and breathless beside him,
"What is that taint, the odor?" "Coyotes," he answered,
"The men shoot them and hang them up on the fence,
Yesterday's by last year's. Come into the field rather
than pass them.
Here there's a gap." He stood until she crept through,
Thinking "Yes: if she enters," and, "I am stone, stone,
I have not trembled.
If I kept the bondage of common men:" he breathed: "to
whom this act would reek like the wire-hung carrion:
I have got outside of good and evil, it needs a symbol,
God thinks through action: when I cried on the
hill,
Love is more cruel than a wolf, hungrier than flame or
the gape of water; your virtues, your nerves, your
goodness,
Rags for that fire." He took April by the arm
Gently, to hasten her steps on the sloping stubble;
She felt herself diminished to helpless childhood, the
ancient
Tower of authority, the trustfulness without thought
Long out of mind: yet the surface of her mind

Insisted "We have come far enough, father.
You were going to tell me . . ." He said eagerly "I'll
     tell you.
But all my thoughts are turbid, like a weighted river
Drops its grain standing, must walk, you'd never under-
     stand
Unless I tell you everything. I have given my mind to
     the future
In love, in love." She stumbled on a stone in the field,
Felt his hand bear her and saw the chip of bent moon
Slip like a silver feather between cloud and sea-fog.
He thought "She is weak and not strong," he said "But
     at best
You won't understand until you follow. I have gone out
     of the maps, it is not written in a book.
I gave myself to find out God, I have found him.
There's yet one link to be filed. Filed." He walked
     faster. "You wouldn't ask me
To love backward, back toward the dead, dead souls:
     April
There's an old dead man under the farmhouse roof,
His horse fell on him and broke him, he lies in bed there
Breathing and dead, they can't bury him still breathing.
To-night there are two corpses lying in the farmhouse.
There is nothing after death. Nothing. You put her
     to bed.
A man who can find God one moment, only one living
     moment, has lived immortally—but how could you
Understand me?—the after is trash. I have come to
     that summit.
I have long ago forgotten sacking my fears
Like blind puppies, a stone for an anchor at the black
     bottom."
She thought "There is one man I never need fear,

Not though he runs mad," her hand nursing
The terrified quick clamor of her heart, and she said,
"But, father,
You asked me to bring her." "I, summon the dead?
Oh, I remember,
To the word with all the black crystals in it, what's the
word? Annihilation, the beautiful crystal contriv-
ance
To catch rays from outside the stars in. We split the
graves. April,
The stone has its nature, but a man
May become God. How could a man touch him or see
him but becoming him? I was on the mountain and
I saw him."
She answered, the words tripping on breaths like sobs:
"It is time.
What have you brought me out here for? I am fright-
ened. Father,
We must go back. I'll take her back home." "Oh
blind,"
He answered letting her arm free, "can't you see the
ocean
Raised like a great black column opposite the hills . . ."
"The rock of Point Sur,
Father, the light above it . . ." "The ocean," he said,
"on one side, the hills on the other, witnessing
The terrible honor, the sacrifice, the marriage of God.
The stars over the cloud-scud
Divided into two antiphonies: April the silver trumpets,
the wailing and singing, the waves
Of answers, the clear, clear voices . . . There is nothing
To be kept and see him, but burn and flame and burn up
All the withdrawals, the evasions, all that feels pain or
shame, the rags of virtues, the dog's meat sanity,

[78]

The blood from the bitten-out arteries . . ." She twist-
ing her hands,
Striking them together, the lips retracted, the teeth
lightening in the dark of her face,
The moon was down, under few stars: "Oh indeed, in-
deed father.
I know that it's all true but you will have pity
And tell me to-morrow, I'm tired, near fainting . . ."
"Was I not tired
The time wandering I found him?" "Dear tired father,"
She panted quickly "but now happy you have found
him.
Now rest and sleep on the hill, I shall not be afraid
Walking alone, the way's easy to the house,
It's very near by, they could hear secrets." "Oh" he
said opposing her,
"You never walked in a path, neither under walls,
Under still hills nor by shining water but hurried breath-
less
To this pole of the world, it was not possible for you
To turn out of it, not possible to flee away from it, did
never voices
Tell you like singing fires, and you looked up at mid-
night and saw wings astonishing the darkness?
As for me I remember drifting the stars before these
Into their ways to make this moment." He stood in
her way
Seeming grown mountainous, such a great mask her fear
Projected on the pitiful human proportions.
She sobbing he said hoarsely, "Panting and hot-blooded
What boy was it last, Edward's gone? You think me
an old man
Daren't dabble in the honeycomb." The treacherous
blood

Now when all needed draining down from her brain
Dimmed the eyes, all the peripheral field of vision
Drawn with a veined gray veil, the colored veins in it
Writhing like serpents, but in the midst as through
    water
The bearded mask darkening against the dim cloud
Was clear enough; she reeled turning but his power
    circled her,
And fallen on the dark, captive: "No matter what horror
Writhes in your mind like worms I am not afraid of you,
You will stop at madness. No matter if hell," she said
    faintly,
Leering faces, cold pads with no claws, soft hairless
    bodies,
Pale tongues bushed with wet hair passed in her mind
Processional, "had struck the gates with broken hinges
And snapped bolts of your mind and entered you like
    conquerors"—
She felt the degradation of resisting his hands,
Dimly, through waves of deep abominable water—
"It could not rule you, oh not to poison the innocent
Years before you went mad. Ah. No. Struck hatchet
In the new-born skull would have been gentle and
    fatherly;
But spit poison in the fountain:" "God has come home
    to you,"
He said furiously, "to you that refused him
Faith, now you feel his power and believe. You laughed
    in your pride
But God is stronger." She struck at the beard, scream-
    ing,
And the night perished about her into horrible sleep,
From which opening she watched a shadow pass crying
And the clouds gone, the gimlet stars all agleam,

And like waves in a grain-field alternate waves
Of bright and dim wore slowly over the whole sky,
Aldebaran, the anthill Pleiades; she felt dull pain
Like a close element, closed eyes, the waves continued
Audible, she hadn't known the sea was so near;
The night was so cold that she would turn on her side
And strive to creep a little toward the house. "I was
     unhappy
A long while before." The waves of starlight, the waves
Of sickness, the long waves of the surf's noise, the cold
     stubble
Undulating . . . When she got up she was able
To walk back to the house; the door was not locked;
No horror behind it. "I am not horrible if nobody
Knows that I am: if I keep it:" her mind had not moved
From torpor before, flashed into bitter activity
Striking its length at random like a burnt snake.
A cataract of phantasmal images filled it
Between the door and the stair; two triumphed and
     remained:
A vision of her own naked body forever
Knotted on the secret scar, her hands crushing
The joined thighs, her nails entering the fruitlike flesh;
And out of the poisoned past of childhood her brother's,
Her dead brother's falsetto fury, "I'd like to kill him.
Oh, Oh if he'd die. I didn't ask to be born.
Be grateful for it, be grateful!"

                       Though   her   mother
     half awoke,
April was able to gather her change of clothing
From the hand-bag in the darkness and hide the stained
     ones.

XIV

An old man on a tired pony rode down the coast
By the distant farms, he said that about midnight
Riding out of the redwoods up the Sur Hill,
Hoping to sleep with Johnny Allado at the shack
On the Hayworth ranch, he heard at a bend feet, hooves,
Hushed voices, a whole company marched in the dark.
He thought, smugglers of liquor bringing it north from
    a landing,
He'd best clear out of the road, and rammed his pony
Into the bushes; there might have been ten went by
Or hundreds, how could he tell, the twigs in his ears?
But someone called from the company, "Oye Mendoza,"
In Spanish, "tell all you meet that our master goes up
To Pico Blanco to be united with God."
Another answered, "Tell him to come;" but the first:
"We have messengers in the north." He heard after-
    wards
A voice in English, he could not tell what it said.
After they'd all gone by he rode to the ranch
And woke Allado. Johnny had gone in the morning
The trail up the South Fork, but himself had come
    south.

At Morhead's Joe Medina heard it and rode
To the ruinous cabin under the limestone ridge
Where his friend Onorio Vasquez the vision-seer

Had camped the nights of a week. The blanket and the
    tins
Were gone, Vasquez was gone. Medina rode home
To coax from the Indian house-girl, Maruca, who loved
    him,
Bread and cold meat; then followed toward the south
    fork
Of the Little Sur River, toward Pico Blanco.
                                    Natalia Morhead
Eyed at noon his vacant place at the table,
"Where's Joe?" And the other farmhand wiping his
    mouth:
"Homesick, I guess. Haven't seen him since breakfast."
"He needn't come back," she said angrily. "To-morrow
Randal comes home: Oh if I could have kept the place
    running
Till Randal . . ." She saw over the table Faith Heriot's
Eyes like light blue flints in the narrow whiteness,
And faltered, and then taking them fairly: "Is grand-
    father
Glad?" Faith, low-voiced: "He hasn't told me, but I
    think
Old grandfather loves Randal as much as I do.
Not any more." Natalia turned from her and anxiously
Fondling the child by her side, "Oh but he'll laugh
To see what a big girl it's grown to: sweetheart when
    he tells you
About the air-planes, the guns and all the soldiers.
Daddy coming to-morrow." Faith Heriot had laid
Iron on her nerves, and after a moment to April Barclay
Said quietly, but the lips like stretched threads, "Your
    father
Isn't at the table either; he wasn't at breakfast."
April, her wound much too deep to feel probing,

Her face not whitened a shade around the great bruise
On the right cheek: "He told me he had work to think
out.
Any farm in the hills will feed him for money.
He walks and works instead of sleeping." She heard
her own voice
Formed and steady as the slender shaft of a pillar,
And felt her face like polished marble and felt perfectly
With quiet and secure attention the shambles under
The marble crust, explosive corruption vaulted with
marble,
"If he were here I'd get him to fix the porch step
That's rotted away, I tripped on last night in the dark,
Coming in, and struck my face on the post." Her mother
Trembled over her private cistern of bitterness,
Ignorant and afraid, feeling the strain, the strain,
The stone faces: "Oh, if Mr. Morhead's coming
We must go home, April; though father's gone off
And I haven't seen him . . ." She imagined April had
spoken
To her father about his madness; and he in what
frenzy—
Ah, had he struck April?—had rushed off in the
night . . .
"Though I haven't seen him . . ." But April unmoved:
"Till father
Comes back, we'll not go away." She knew herself rock
To stay to the end: for what reason was dark:
No reason: it was resolved. "If Mr. Morhead
When he comes wants us to leave we'll get the Hay-
worths
To keep us." She thought "They'll wonder." She
thought "My secret's
Horrible enough to be safe: and if it had happened

That's unbelievable: Oh clearly all one's desire
Would be to flee, to flee, to forget: to wait here
Locks it rather." She said "Here we must wait,
When he wants to see mother he'll find us." She felt
Unguessed continents of fortitude. But none was needed
Where nothing hurt much, nothing now was intolerable,
This puddle of slime and blood excessive, in the infinite
    ocean?
The shores had been set wider.
Whatever needed to be done would be done: herself
Not responsible: there stood a competent power
Running the machine. The world in a moment so
    changed
Utterly . . . She felt the sweat cold on her forehead,
The sight of the eyes narrowing again and the sweat
Trickle down from the throat between the two
    breasts . . .
She caught herself back: since no fortitude sufficed
Flayed with the nails of her right hand the wrist of her
    left
Under the table, caught herself back from falling
On faintness . . . not faintness, the silken-curtained, a
    new
State of consciousness, without brakes, without rudder,
Might have involved confession: she took it captive
And retained rule, thinking of Edward her brother,
Why did his face and shoulders rise up? She raised up
Her head, and her eyes warred on Faith Heriot's.
    Natalia's
Always went down humbled: Faith Heriot's went down
But not humbled. "We'll stay though."

                                        At the foot of
        Pico Blanco mountain
                [85]

Barclay had stumbled on black exhaustion, he turned
  on his followers,
The five or six Onorio Vasquez had gathered to follow
  him: "It is finished. Let me go. Nothing remains.
You have no conception," he cried, striking his fists
  against his eyes, "of the treachery of—what's his
  name?—God, God.
But if you have led me into this wilderness to kill me—
  do it quickly. Oh mercy, mercy! I am not pre-
  pared.
Who knows there is nothing afterwards?" Onorio Vas-
  quez
To the others: "He is only a man, he must see God.
No man could come up to it and not go mad with terror.
Go down to the creek and make camp." Barclay had
  staggered
To his knees and babbled, bending his forehead earth-
  ward, "Have pity. Oh, oh.
I was so hurried on from madness to madness
I never had choice, I was rushed down to destruction."
He said picking at the earth, "They wove it too loose,
All full of eye-holes, the horror steams up through it.
Hunted out of life. No refuge. Oh cheat, cheat!"
    They watched him,
And Vasquez took a fallen branch of dead oak
And struck at them though it broke in his hand, and
  drove them
Down hill from the path. "Go and make camp by the
  creek.
When it's time, then I will call you." He said, "Master,
  my prophet,
Sleep." But he grovelling on the blind earth: "To
  murder me!
Oh, oh, have mercy," and fought to rise and fell down

On the white trail under the high sun in the dust of
limestone.
He seemed sleeping and moaning. Then Vasquez cut
poles
And slanted them over his head from southward to the
oak-bough
And spread the shelter of a blanket.

In the afternoon
Came a few riders from the coast and went down to the
brook
At Vasquez' word. The sun approached the Sur Hill
Burning laces of cloud; eastward above the ridges mush-
room-capped giants
Of cotton-white cloud piled and rose higher. Then
Barclay
Moved and cried out under the tent of the blanket.
When Vasquez drew it down from the poles he said, "I
am Lazarus,
I was taking water to the women in the fire." Vasquez
made haste
And brought him water in a can; he spilled it on the
earth,
And the young man brought it again he drank and said
quietly, "Nothing is forgotten.
The sun falls against evening and rain in November.
The dead are quiet, I was only dreaming."

The people
Had seen Vasquez go down for water and return.
They came from the creek saying, "It is late. Has he
wakened?"
Three others coming the trail from the coast each party
in the other
Saw multitude at the mountain-foot.

[87]

XV

Then Barclay: "I have come to the mountain.
None of you knows over what pass I have come, over
what white ridge . . . prone like a beast . . .
clinging,
When I cast my hands and my love over the future in
the ecstasy: threw forward: changed times like
God . . . nor what
Sacrifice bled on the hill.
I told you what God requires: the tragic child gashing
himself with knives in the ecstasy, to discover
New shores and there is nothing but himself: trying all
the ways and chances forever, tortured from eter-
nity;
Himself the furnace, himself the God, himself the burnt-
offering: I will break up my memory, it is finished,
And not remember this thing, it is finished. . . . You
scum of the coast
What wave carried you up here? How did the waters
turn backward, you and the lean horses? I had
many companions
Before."
                    And certainly when they looked about them
The ridges were filled, the woods in the south over the
canyon
With listeners, the trail they had come from the ocean

With eyes and mouths, the long ridge eastward with
    erect
Multitude, men like trees against the standing
Domes and caverns of cloud; only the mountain-slope
Naked. And now the day's eyeball was hidden,
The shadow of the Sur Hill lay over the valley,
The white peak blazed.
                      "But I will make promises for
    God. He desires not only
Destruction, but more than the fire feeding on the eyes,
    than the knives pastured on flesh: power, power,
    and the terrible
Buds of growth in the bone sepulchres the slime of
    your brains
Stuffs with lazy corruption: I tell you there is soil
    under the lock of those arches, spear-rooted fire
Will suck it and take heaven.
I have the burning to kindle you. I tell you that the
    brown bodies and the white bodies of you cheap
    counters,
You pawns, you unregarded droppets of chance-blown
    wombs, are the seeds of the world
I am planting between to-night and to-morrow: the hand
    plucking the sun for its apple, the bridle of the
    hand
Of a man on the last planet, the huge capture, humanity
    taking its house, the final possession."
They understood nothing but listened. It seemed to
    them all he was making magic in the shadow of
    the air
With speech incomprehensible and ancient gestures, and
    the hurricane his mind. "Stopped eyes, me use
    you? I will tell you

In the talk that will touch you in the bone caves.   I
    know that I stand near God and speak for him.

He brought me from the north; I was fifty years old, I
    am ageless

He gave me sap of redwoods to drink, towers of millen-
    nial

Inexhaustible life, I shall be young still

A thousand years from this day, nothing can weary me.

He gave me the strength to endure . . . mountains: and
    the power

To move them: the power to take possession

Of the blind throats and stopped channels—

Brute material—that rages in the air over your heads
    like a wind

Nursing lightning.   And knowledge he gave me, that
    stands against the fountain and touches the stir of
    currents

Before they are streams; the intent moves in his depth

And is born cauled in clear flame to be stars

And new structures of suns, and vermin on the planets;
    I tasted it

In the germ of the egg, I, here, I am his token

And symbol to you that he will give you these gifts,

Inexhaustible life, incomparable power, inhuman knowl-
    edge:

That he will make you Gods walking on the earth

And striking the sky.

                    I preach promises to rats: I will
    tell you in the squeak of your private voices: you
    are poor,

He will make you rich, give you the deeds to valleys of
    meat and cattle and mined gold in the mountains.

You love drunkenness: he will fill you with wine that
never sickens nor runs empty. You want women:
he will make you
All beautiful and young, sweet-smelling: carved and
delicate girls of ivory and gold will creep to your
feet
Trembling, begging to be stabbed. You will choose new
for each night,
Virgins: and it will not be sin but honesty, you must
people the earth
That shall be emptied to be new: I tell you I have seen
in the fountain of God destruction standing
With stone hooves on the cities, he will trample and
burst all but my chosen, he will sweep them with
brooms of pestilence,
Scrub them with fire: I heard him whistle the black dog
Death to lick out the dish: but you that come to me
Shall watch from secure hills and not weep."
                                    He thought
        in himself, "Madness, madness,
And lies: it is put in my mouth."
                                    He said: "I am taking
        up to this mountain the private
Desire like a jewel of each of you, to give to the infinite
Power, and I know that he will give you fulfilment."
        He turned to go up the mountain. "But you
        Onorio
Shepherd them to-night." He walked upward in the
        shadow of the twilight, limestone burned rose above
        him and faded,
The eagle light ebbed from the cloud.

XVI

April, in the house,
Had never moved but struck her forehead against im-
prisonment.
The presence of her mother was the most oppressive.
She would have walked alone in the fields but the field
Was Tarquin, and the small pain of walking a new
deflowerment.
"Mother, let's take the car and go down to the sea.
I am dead in this house." Audis would have refused,
But thought "If he should come back and I should be
alone."
But April was thinking "If we should meet him on the
road.
Or be together in the car and meet him by the sea."
Their eyes crossing it seemed to her struck a dull spark
Of loathsome shared wisdom, like the offspring monkey
Of old diseases, for she thought "We have shared
Knowledge of a man, were virgin under one violence,
We harem-sisters," the explosive corruption
Straining the polished vault-stones.
But the chief strain,
the strain,
Was lower than consciousness, her mind was filmed over
it.
"Only a maniac: not the same man: have been handled
By a mad beast and life will grow over the horror

Kept secret and sealed shut." They passed the thick-
furred
Coyotes hung heads downward on the wire fence
Corrupting the air; the freshest corpse had its ears,
The heads of the others had been gnawed; two hawks
hung by them.
And April easily: "Vermin they shoot and hang there
To warn the others, I suppose." They came to the
wide sand-flat,
And looked across it at the great rock of Point Sur
That carries the little-seeming lighthouse buildings.
They found a track northward to a shore of cliffs
And inlet sands. Audis remained in the car,
April went down to a coved beach, the low sun
Burnt the sea gold. Lying on the pure sand
She felt the strain loosened, the strain slid over
Into sweet reveries.
                She did not think to herself
These were new dreams and not a girl's dreams, an
adolescent
Boy's, that made windy honey in her mind. A dark
prow swung in the sun's track;
Erect sword-slender figure riding the plunge of the great
prow toward Asia.
(Travelling needs money: a madman soon dies, I shall
have money.) But why do you wander into wide
Asia?
To ride the desert horses under the Mongol stars, all
night to ride horses.
The enormous plain slips like a ribbon, the stars follow
like birds in the trough of the sky, the flowing
Of the sheet muscles in the great shoulders. Dawn
builds an awful flower at the world's end. I shake
the black tents.

[93]

Again and again you desert horsemen
Have raided the world and there was nothing but fell
    down.
Wild riders, you have forgotten Attila,
You have not forgotten Genghiz, is Tamerlane for-
    gotten?
The world is full of filth and despair,
I am welding you tribes into the sword that will
    straighten it.
I have taken my inheritance from my father
To buy you guns, you will bring me the spoil of
    provinces.
My parents have eaten corrupt food and my throat was
    defiled, the man whom I called father had gone
    mad.
If I had a dog that was fallen into the pit would I not
    save him? *I ended my father's madness.*
I will tell you a secret.
That beast with the brown beard was not my father.
That dead man not my father: but he had gone mad,
He could not have lived. What wandering poet
In her bride youth in the moon of beauty
That shines once on every woman
Sang me into the womb of my mother?
They whispered in the garden. But I have a sword for
    a song, wild tribesmen . . .

                        Audis above
Stood on the cliff against the white cloud, and calling
"April, how long? April." But April to herself:
"She is calling my sister, I need not answer." And
    Audis,
"Are you asleep April? I see you on the sand."
Then April let the revery hang in suspense
And answered, "It's me, mother, April's not here,

It's Edward," she was about answering, and suddenly
The strain and the desecration of being herself
Came like a wave. She rose and went up to her mother,
The earth and the sea swayed, she mounted the rocks.
When she remembered, she thought she had been pos-
  sessed
By her brother Edward's spirit returned from death.
The sun was like a red bead on a wire
Flat on the sea. The desecration; the strain,
The strain. "Though I am wrong-sexed, defenceless
  mother,
I'll be her sword and her son." To have thought so,
  eased
The strain, the strain; but nothing to be said out loud;
It was necessary to live in tunnels of secrecy.
"But I am new-sexed, mother needs help, Edward is
  dead,"
She confused Edward and her father, "he is dead."

XVII

And when Natalia came in the evening and spoke
Of Randal her husband coming to-morrow, released
From the dead war and service, April thought "Edward
Released from service: to-day Edward came back;
The other is coming to-morrow"; it was part of the
    strain
That strands tangled and metals melted together;
Nothing was ever pure in her mind, one wave at a time
Might be swum through, but always the battering
    alliance;
She kept herself calm in the face, paying silence for it,
Until she felt the tears flooding her eyelids,
Flowing down the bruised cheek and the other, then
    sobs
Wrenched her throat. "You are happy," she said. And
    the other,
"Oh what have I done to hurt you?" "Nothing, noth-
    ing.
My brother was killed. I cry easily, I'm tired to the
    bones . . ."
Natalia with a sudden pitying affection
Kissed her and stroked the short brown hair.
                                        Faith Heriot
Stood on the stair and looked down, shaking, and the
    oval
Face like the foam-lantern on a night wave.

"You're soon friendly. Don't mind, Miss . . . Barclay,
     she always
Handles newcomers lovingly—me—me,
Two years ago. And her fellow's coming to-morrow,
It flows over all syrupy." Natalia drew back
Like guilt, and April gazing from one to the other
Thought of her father's horrible . . . love.
The air had flecks of fire in it and flecks of slime,
She thought how this one and the other drop dung in the
     mornings,
And yet affectionate animals . . . "Live in steel
     towers,"
She thought silently, "horrible to smell each other,
To touch each other," and said, "I am not in your com-
     pany,
Keep your endearments for each other," yet passing
     between them
She realized through the loathing the terrible beauty,
The white and moulded, the hot lightnings under the
     cloth,
The beastlike sucking bodies as beautiful as fire,
The fury of archangelic passions, her eyes
Having changed sex a moment. She whispered on the
     stair
"Oh, burn, never grow old; burn, burn." The ungeared
Mind ran wild in the sad bed by her mother
Through phantasmal pollutions and lightning beauty
Like a child screaming in a labyrinth; toward dawn,
     sleep
Sealed it with lead.
                    I say that if the mind centers on
          humanity
And is not dulled, but remains powerful enough to feel
     its own and the others, the mind will go mad.

[97]

It is needful to remember the stone and the ocean, without the hills over the house no endurance,
Without the domed hills and the night. Not for quietness, not peace;
They are moved in their times. Not for repose; they are more strained than the mind of a man; tortured and twisted
Layer under layer like tetanus, like the muscles of a mountain bear that has gorged the strychnine
With the meat bait: but under their dead agonies, under the nightmare pressure, the living mountain
Dreams exaltation; in the scoriac shell, granites and basalts, the reptile force in the continent of rock
Pushing against the pit of the ocean, unbearable strains and weights, inveterate resistances, dreams westward
The continent, skyward the mountain . . . The old fault
In the steep scarp under the waves
Melted at the deep edge, the teeth of the fracture
Gnashed together, snapping on each other; the powers of the earth drank
Their pang of unendurable release and the old resistances
Locked. The long coast was shaken like a leaf. April Barclay
Came from blind lakes of sleep, her mother was laboring
At the locked door, but April in the shaken darkness
Imagined her father breaking entrance and cried out
In a boy's voice, feeling in her hands already
The throat under the beard, but whispering, "Oh mother,
Don't tremble so." She had slipped from the bed and she felt
The floor under her feet heave and be quieted.

But Audis through her terror had heard the sparrows
Cry out in the oak by the window, in the leonine roar
Of the strained earth, the clatter of bricks or small
    stones,
And the great timbers of the walls grind on their bear-
    ings.

XVIII

Barclay on the mountain.

He had climbed under the glaze of the lost red sundown

And under the moments of the cloud-wandering moon;
    but after dense cloud

Covered the mountain, was no recourse nor higher in
    the savage darkness. He had found a ledge of
    slant rock

Where one could take three paces and return three paces,
    always fondling the cliff, remembering the precipice.

Here his faith died. While the eyes of belief

Had fed him, standing above those followers at the foot
    of the mountain, he had almost believed

Power would indeed visit him, at night, on the mountain.

But now across the dreadful emptiness of sanity re-
    turned a moment, in the solid dark, the vertiginous

Absection, with clear weak voice only the mind,

That merest phantom, no power of the flesh supporting
    it, no emotion, repeated

That there is one power, you may call it God to the
    vulgar,

Exists from eternity into eternity, all the protean phe-
    nomena, all forms, all faces of things,

And all the negligible lightnings of consciousness,

Are made of that power . . . What did it matter? out-
    side communication, nowise adorable, not touch-
    able

But in the minutest momentarily formed and dissolving
    fractions: rock . . . flesh . . . phenomena!   the
    unhappy
Conception closes the circle back to its beginning,
Nothing discovered in all the vicious circumference.
"At least no guilt nor judgment discovered: I am free
    of the phantasy
That has wrecked giants. None. No regret. None."
But the mind with a twist of insane cunning: "There is
    one Power,
You may call it God to the vulgar. How shall men live
Without religion? All the religions are dead,
When it stank you denounced it. You are chosen to
    found the new one,
To draw from your own fountain the soul of the world.
What did you expect, the God would show himself vis-
    ibly, his voice roar, his hand cover you in a cranny
    of the rock
Against the flaring eyes soul-eating terror the unbearable
    face,
And let you peep at his rump when the power passes?"
He crouched wearily at the end of the ledge. "This lie
    or a like one
To cram the mouth of credulity when I return to them.
One must paint pictures, no faith's honest at the stalk.
The night on the mountain will not be useless; the
    prophet
Not his own dupe." The clouds that drowned the star-
    light kept the night warm.
The solid and secure darkness. He half slept, and April
Went by in a dream, the region and the blood of de-
    flowerment
Bright through her torn clothing; she smiled with wise
    eyelids.

Then Barclay felt the torpor drop off líke a cloak,
Like a cloud split with lightning . . . certainly this
    cloud
Has lightning in it, he felt it tingle at the hair-roots,
And strain, the strain in the air . . . and he said, "Oh
    Lord God
Why have you deceived me? Why turned me to these?
To be your gull and love them, I will not be your fool
And take their part against you and their part in de-
    struction, they have had their Jesus,
Me also to be hanged on Caucasus?"

                              The region people
Were present in him, his mind contained them, and the
    others,
Innumerable, covering the earth, cities and fields of hu-
    manity, the Americas, Asia, the ravenous
Billion of little hungers, the choked obscene desires, the
    microscopic terrors and pities,
All present in that intolerable symbol his daughter
With the bare bleeding wound in her.

                              "These? Against
    the stars? To what end?
For either the ice will come back and bury them, or the
    earth-crust open and fire consume them,
Or much more likely they will have died of slow-rotting
    age
Millions of years before." The God in his insane mind
Answered: "Is it nothing to you that I have given you
The love and the power? How many times earlier in
    bourneless eternity
Have they not flowered; and you from the violent bath
    heavy with the fury of the love stood evident above
    them,"

He had risen and stood on the rock, "the pillar of the
   bride humanity's desire. The explosion, the pas-
   sion, repeated
Eternally: what if they rot after, you and they shall
   return again. The bride and the bridegroom: the
   unions of fire
Like jewels on a closed necklace burn holes through ex-
   tinction." But he remembering
Crouched on the rock and whispered "There is pain,
   there is terror,
I have heard of torture. The inflictions of disease and
   of men that knot up
Muscles and the screaming nerves into one horror."
   The God in his mind answered, "These also return."
It seemed to Barclay the cloud broke and he saw the
   stars,
Those of this swarm were many, but beyond them uni-
   verse past universe
Flared to infinity, no end conceivable. Alien, alien, alien
   universes. At length, one similar
To this one; instantly his mind crying through the vast-
   ness
Pitched on the twin of this one, the intolerable identical
Face framed in the same disastrous galaxy: and if once
   repeated
Repeated forever. He heard the scream of suffered
   violence on the dark hill; he ate the miracle,
The closed serpent.
   Consciousness drowned and sleep covered him.
                                               In a
   dream a young man
Approached him, what was it they were saying? Ed-
   ward, Edward,

Why does thy brand drip red with blood?   "That's an
    old song
And this is a dream."   He awoke.   On the ledge a young
    man
Approached him.   "We knew by wire, Edward.   The
    telegram
Broke your mother's heart and my mind from that hour
Scrabbles at the doors, April seems not to care much."
Your hawk's blood was never so red . . .
"I am Christ, I have come to slay God who violated my
    mother
And streaked the earth with its pangs."   "God has
    turned.   God loves.   Oh my son
He has taken the people's part against the wild stars."
"The agony," the young man answered,
"I suffered grew from your mind but I will make an
    end.
My crucifixion a digging between the war-lines,
My death-wound in the belly, I licked the wound in
    my arm
Like a dog but in the anguish of thirst for three days."
Your hound's blood was never so dear . . . "That is not
    my reason
That I shall kill you."   "What is it you are hiding
    Edward
In your hand behind your back?"   "All the earth's
    agonies
Scream in my ears like famished eaglets in the aerie
Furious for the black flesh of annihilation.
To be ended and sleep, not to be renewed: that is not
    my reason
That I shall kill you."   The old man: "Oh my son, my
    son,

The enormous beauty of the world!" "It is too much
  to pity,
Too heavy to endure," he answered, "I will make it
  peace;
Too many times having attempted atonement.
That is not my reason." Oh I will kill my father
  dear . . .
The old man: "God lifts his head and laughs in white
  heaven.
When have you considered the stars, what have you
  known of the streams in my soul,
And one lit point lost in the sky's eternity
A universe, millions of many-planeted suns, but another
  a universe
Of universes: they move in my mind, they shine within
  me, they eat infinite renewals." The young man:
"Nailed to the wood of groaning I meditated these
  things,
And seeing as in a vision all the vain bitterness.
I am one with my father, his equal in power, I have
  turned against him.
I did not ask for existence." And Barclay: "I gave you
The gift that the mouth was not yet moulded to ask for
  nor the heart to desire. I am changed, I have
  turned to love men.
I was like a furnace and a raging in the midst of the
  stars. I embraced the future, I came to
  a virgin . . ."
Oh I have killed my father dear. "I," the young man
  answered,
"To even that stabbing love of yours with steel." He
  approached and the hidden right hand
Was drawing from behind his loins, Barclay awoke
  from the dream

[105]

And knew it for one.   There was nothing.   The thick
    darkness
Was like annihilation.   He crouched on the rock whis-
    pering
"No guilt, no judgment, no guilt, for I looked.   There
    was renewal.
Will the dead not be quiet?   Oh horrible, pursue
From one star-grain of sand to another through desert
    eternity?
And if the life is annihilated and memory
Lives . . ."   He imagined the gray hair on his head
Lifting and blanched.   "Having entered annihilation,
The terror at the shoulder after the shoulder has
    crumbled?"
Crouched on the rock he felt his knees knocking to-
    gether
Against his will though he strove at quietness, and then
All his body trembling.
                            The strain, the strain in the
    air.   Come lightning?

The sparrows in the oak at April's window
Cried out.   The fault under the sea had slipped, and
    the people
Camping beside the creek under the mountain
Heard the hills move, heard the woods heaving, the
    boughs of the redwoods
Beating against each other from the southwest,
And the roaring earth.   The earth swayed in waves like
    a bog
Under the strewn boughs they lay on and was quiet.
Certain among the frightened twenty remembered
Their new faith and believed that God had come down

To stand on the clouded mountain. They heard stones
    falling.

Barclay heard the forest and the stones falling
And the roaring earth. He felt the limestone mountain
    shaken
For a willow leaf in a light wind by the streamside.
When the mountain was quiet his body had ceased
    trembling.
He sat in the darkness exalted, shattered with exalta-
    tion,
Considering this thing, feeling his humanity slipped off
Lie on the rock like a skin, like a cast shirt.
"When I trembled in a bad dream: the earth shook when
    I trembled.
The dream knew me by name. It is true. I have touched
    truth."
He did not feel he had been received into communion,
But that he had realized his own members and func-
    tions . . . "All the life, all the power.
All. All the orbits and times."
                                    Silent lightning
Twitched curtains on the edges of heaven and over the
    mountain,
Few flashes, like forms of ceremony. No rain-drops.
Dawn lingered and then triumphed. Barclay came
    down,
His face livid against the streaming splendors of the
    mountain.
He had found the perfect confidence that controls
The faith of followers, but it was hard to remember
In the huge fenceless dispersion, in the torrent and
    weight
Of what appeared universal awareness,

These few followers. When he saw them he thought
    "My secret
Would set me away from them, outside the stars." Vas-
    quez came upward
From the others grouped in the path or running among
    the trees, then Barclay
Seemed to remember Vasquez and made movements of
    speech
Without a voice; he spoke again, audibly, and said:
"Multitude. But I will be with you. If sight or hear-
    ing Onorio,
Or vision, brings you the awful secret, lock it in your
    heart
Not to be spoken." He ate when they brought him
    food.

XIX

At Morhead's place the slender brick chimney
Propped to the roof against the south winds, had broken
Where the roof bound it; the bricks gashed the black
    roof
But slid on the sheathing and rained outward. Faith
    Heriot
Slept under the roof to nurse the bed-bound old man.
She stood on the rocking floor, when the match spurted
The earth had resumed its old passionate quietness.
The old man had his unimpaired; only the eyes
Moved, though the hands were able to. The bleached
    gray eyes
Danced in the matchlight to the dead motion of the
    earth,
And steadied. Faith lighted the lamp, listlessly saying
"The chimney went down," in the tone of a slack ques-
    tion.
He answered in the earthy and dim voice, "Go on down.
She dreamed her husband was home and it shook the
    bedstead.
The old walls I have built have stood more shaking than
    this."
Faith lighted a candle for the stair and went down;
    there was long light
From the end of the hallway, the strangers had made a
    light

And had their door open: she entered Natalia's.
The bed was empty, she heard a murmuring like love
And spilled the grease from the candle turning on the
    darkness,
Her teeth bared. Natalia lay prone
On the child's narrower bed, her shielding body
Over the child's. The white legs and clear arms
Gleamed in the smoky flicker, the drawn night-dress
Moulded the loins, and the mass of black hair
Lay like a stain on the coverlet. Faith trembled and
    touched.
"Get up, it's over. What are you afraid of?" And
    then
Seeing in her mind the phallic shaft of the chimney,
And that it had had to be propped against the south
    storms,
"The chimney went down," she said exultantly, "no
    wonder."
Natalia sat up weeping. "Nothing will be left,
Everything had to be ruined before Randal comes home,
To-morrow: to-day." Faith, shaking, "Let him go back
    then
To the camp women. What he wants." She met the
    child's eyes
Like pools of blue shadow on the pillow and thought
    bitterly,
"If you'd die and be out of it." She said "I lied to you,
Long, long ago." Natalia seemed to grow conscious
Of Faith's presence, her lover's, "dearest, what lie?"
She drew the stretched linen from her knees, it had
    made a bad fold,
Smiled wistfully and straightened the dark forest of
    hair, when suddenly the child
Wailed a long quaver of meaningless desolation,

Her eyes fixed on Faith Heriot. Natalia lifted her;
And Faith submissively: "It's almost morning, let me
stay
Till the light comes; I never shall be able to again."
Natalia murmured to Rachel, who gripped a thick
strand
Of her live hair in the little fingers and slept.
The child and the mother seemed to become one person,
And Faith felt like a hawk blinded at night
Beating on glass. She screwed the hem of her garment
To a twist over the thigh, the stiff white tassel
Seemed to have pitiful significance, she tensed her body
in the chair
With all the strain of writhing violence, not moving
The slender body. Natalia brooded on the child.
There were noises in the house; the mother and the
girl, the strangers,
Must have dressed and gone down. Smells of wood-
smoke and coffee
Cut the night air, the old Chinaman was up and at
work,
Certainly the stove would smoke, was dangerous, no
matter,.
And when the window glimmered to grayness Faith
said,
The child sleeping: "The day I came here
Rachel was sick with fever and you sat
Like this Natalia holding her. She was so little
She remembered the breasts and you had made yourself
bare
To cool her face against them.—Oh," she thought shiv-
ering,
"To strangle the dawn, destroy movements and per-
sons,

[111]

The strain," and she said quietly, "The earth finds hap-
piness
When it stretches and shakes after it is tired being
quiet. You smiled pitifully
But all my blood ran on my heart when I saw you.
I couldn't have helped touching your shoulder dearest.
You said that when I touched you the baby's breathing
Changed and the forehead was wet, the fever was gone.
Yes, into *me!*" Natalia peacefully: "I loved you
Because Rachel got well after you touched me. What
was the lie
You said you told me, was it then?" "If I tell you,
You'd make me go away, I'll never go away."
She stood like a thin white pillar in the room. "What
right have you
To be so rich and so happy? What right have you
to have three? I had one,
And to-day takes you."
She moved in the room like a thin jet of white fire.
"What time does he come
And slobber on your mouth, morning?" Natalia,
Turned ice, answered, "I don't want you in my room.
And if the house is hateful to you, go out of it.
The rats feel the ship stagger; Medina went yesterday,
The ship will swim yet." Faith answered, "I cannot en-
dure to-day,
But what shall I do when night comes?" She covered
her face
With the hooked fingers. Natalia, turning to pity,
Laid down the child on the bed, but Faith: "When I felt
it,
I prayed it tremble harder and shake down the hung
floors
And roll the old trees of the walls over us dead,

[112]

A butt on each brain. It was not my father."
Natalia, shrewd-eyed: "What was not?"   "The man
    that had me.
I was ashamed that anyone else . . . Oh, be careful.
Have you forgotten that I had a softer sex
Before my misery, and might again."   "Who was it?"
    "Be careful.
He had furred me inside with life, my mother had cancer
In the same fountain. She took me to Monterey,
Going to the hospital to be saved.
She lied to my father, she paid the doctor for mine,
Had my sickness clawed out. Something went wrong.
The smell of the ether makes me sick to remember."
"Why did you tell me the monstrous . . ."   "My father
    came up
Unexpected: found me where my mother
Ought to have been. He took my mother and went home.
Now I don't know whether she lives or is dead.
I had to leave the hospital three days later,
The money was gone. I took the stage to go home,
I believed father would kill me. I had to walk
From where the stage left me."   "You fell in the road
Outside the door. I made Maruca bring you in.
Little Rachel had the fever. Why did you make the lie
About your father?"   "Not to go back to the lighthouse.
So that you wouldn't send me home to him, I hate him.
It came in my mind."   "Then who was the man that—"
    "Ah, no,"
She answered, the face wrinkling, "my shame's my own
    still."
Natalia trembled, she thought of Randal's absences,
Her husband's, the weeks before he entered the army,
When he used to wander seaward toward the rock at
    Point Sur,

[113]

Then suddenly without reason enough he enlisted,
They'd never have drafted him: Faith was in trouble at
    that time.
He'd not been gone two weeks and Rachel got sick;
He'd just been gone a month Faith Heriot fell fainting
In the road at the door.
                  Neither Natalia nor Faith
Understood how the anguish of desertion, and the
    mother's sacrifice,
The penalizing pain and weakness, had changed
Faith's nature, who'd been punished not be caught twice,
Not again suffer this misery. Drowned under conscious-
    ness
That resolution: and furious envy of the man,
The sex that only inflicted, not suffered: the tropic na-
    ture
Knowing that no fence would cage it found the other
    outlet.
She had found Natalia, young, hot, husband-forsaken,
Beautiful to be wooed: Faith had learned something
From school-girl friends in town, when her father kept
    the light at Point Pinos:
And the sweet furnace painted with natural friendship,
And at the furnace heart the jewel sterility,
The love without fear.
                Her nature sea-streams
Set in new ways poured on the openings of Eden,
She never had acknowledged happiness before.
                    But now she cried out
So that the child Rachel awoke on the bed
Sobbing. She cried: "I wish it had shaken the ocean
Over all standing heights and everything alive.
I wish the hills opened their doors and streamed fire,
    when it struck the ankles

The hands would fall in, and when the wrists were
  burnt through, the faces. I wish that it darkened
Toward the last night instead of pinching out the last
  day
Like a peeled snake." Natalia forgot the child sobbing
And ranged white through the room gathering her day-
  clothes
With picking fingers. She heaped them in a place.
  And Faith Heriot:
"It's good that he comes, time to give up and be quiet,
People can't live like this. Dear friend. Dear friend.
I could show you something.
If you'd a little knife and you'd nick me here
On the arm or anywhere: melted stone would run out.
There's no common red left. What it feels like." The
  child
Cried, and Natalia handled the heap of clothing.
But then with the gesture of a diver long balanced
Above chill water, who plunges, she slipped the night-
  dress
Over the dark-forested head, and Faith Heriot
Saw the arms lifted, the nippled moons, the white-
  moulded
Erect caryatid slenderness waver on slant dawn
A moment before it stooped to be clouded: she felt
A change like death and tears tracked the white cheeks,
She whispered, "I will be quiet, oh, I'll be quiet.
I had no right." She leaned to the door and fumbled
The knob with shaking fingers. "Be happy. I'll stay
  up-stairs.
I haven't forgotten the old quietness upstairs. *My*
  baby.
The only log of the house that needs feeding. Oh."
  She fled out.

XX

The day brought home Randal to the house and Barclay
    to the hill,
The one believing himself happy and the other
Believing himself God. Barclay remembered
The empty cabin under the limestone ridge;
There would abide a season; his following people
Took the hillside; they were not few, now the long coast
Was couriered north and south with extravagant stories
Of powers and wonders; he was said to have prophesied
    the earthquake,
Have foretold future destructions, and have healed sick
    folk.
But many during the next days came up to him
To find amusement, it was slack of the year on the steep
    farms,
The plows waiting for rain.
                        Onorio Vasquez
Passed among the hundred with screaming visions.
Onorio and one of his brothers, and two women
The madness touched, went in and out of the cabin
Seeing Barclay, who kept quietness, and feeding him.
    Toward evening the second day
Barclay went up among the people to the white ridge;
    and standing above them:
"I have sent the other multitude away. I have put them
    in my left hand. I will show you the face of God.

He is like a man that has an orchard, all the boughs
    from the river to the hill bending with abundance,
Apples like globes of sunset, apples like burnt gold from
    the broken mountain: . . . the man is a madman.
He has found a worm in one of the apples: he has turned
    from all the living orchard to love the white worm
That pricks one apple. I tell you," he said, writhing
    above them, "that God has gone mad.
What, here on this one fruit, lump of earth-sprinkled
    stone
With the iron core, this earth you call it,
There's noble to love: if these mountains were not enough
    he has mountains under the south, the condor-
Nesting Andes, and in Asia Himalaya
Shining like candles before sunrise hung socketless
In the night of the air: he has turned away from them,
    he has gone mad, he has turned to love men. You
    greasy foreheads,
It is not for power nor beauty, what have you got under
    you that I should love you? The cut blue crystal,
    the ocean,
Has brilliance on its face and broken shadows and shin-
    ings, and in the heart silence: it is set in the conti-
    nents
For the gold band, it is like the great jewel of the ring.
    He has turned and left it, he has turned to love
    men,
I tell you God has gone mad, he has broken
The ring not of the earth but eternity, he has broken
    his eternal nature: so a doomed man
Changes his mould of nature, a month before death, the
    miser scatters the gold counters, the coward
Eats courage somewhere. If he needed flesh
To spend that passion on . . ."

One of the women
flung herself on the rock
Under his feet, crying "Lord, I am here," and moaning
    anxiously.   Her work-worn hands dug the rough
    stone;
Her prostrate body, ridged with the thrusting corset-
    bones, like a broken machine
Twitched out its passion.
                        Barclay continued not look-
    ing downward: "Must he love cellular flesh, the
    hot quivering
Sheathed fibers, the blood in them,
And threaded lightning the nerves: had he no choice,
    are there not lions in the nights of Africa
Roar at his feet under the thunder-cloud manes?   Not
    hawks and eagles, the hooked violence between
The indomitable eyes, storms of carnivorous desire drive
    over the huge blue?   He has chosen insanely, he
    has chosen
The sly-minded, the cunning-handed, the talkative-
    mouthed,
The soft bodies go shelled in cloth: he has chosen to
    sheathe his power in women, sword-strike his pas-
    sion
In the eyes of the sons of women. . . . I cannot tell you
    what madness covered him; he heard a girl's
    voice . . ."   Barclay
Shook like a fire and cried out: "I am not ready to call
    you.
Let no one come to me, no one be moved."   He stood
    rigid above them, like a man struck blind, feeling
The spheres of fire rushing through the infinite room in
    the bubble of his mind: but hearing inward his
    prophet

[118]

Onorio Vasquez, clamoring across the people:
"The April-eyed, the daughter," he cried in his vision,
"And the honey of God,
Walks like a maiden between the hills and high waters,
She lays her hand passing on the rock at Point Sur,
The petals of her fingers
Curve on the black rock's head, the lighthouse with
      lilies
Covered, the lightkeepers made drunken like bees
With her hand's fragrance . . ."

                            Faith Heriot had
        come up alone,
Her laughter like a knife ran over the people, "Old
      Heriot
My father in the lily fragrance, the cowhide face
Drunken in the lilies." And Onorio: "I see the long
      thighs,
Pillars of polished lightning, the marbled flanks
That God made to desire: she is not a maiden, she is all
      humanity,
The breasts nippled with faces, the blue eyes
Dizzy with starlight: Oh blue wells
Of sorrow, he will brim you with rejoicing, Oh bruised
      lips,
The God of the stars crushed with his kiss . . ."

                                      Bar-
        clay like trumpets
Crossing a hawk's cry: "Only by force I have held
      off you
The meteor death plunging at the eyes that dared see
      and the mouth prophesy
What the stars cloud from. For your faith I saved
      you."

                  [119]

He said to the others: "It is true: I threw forward: he
  has seen.
I take youth to my age. I threw forward and struck
  talons in the future, I have spat out the mother
And left Eve in the dust of the garden. Where's
  Cæsar, where is Jesus, what have I to do with dead
  men?
The unborn are my people and you are my people, Ah,
  love,
I am breeding falcons. No fear that your new lover
  will expiate his passion
On lightning-prodded Caucasus under the vultures,
On the earthquake-rocked cross. The power and the
  love have joined, the great God is the lover, he has
  parted the stars
Like leaves to come at love. Be silent, stand quiet, I
  will not have you
Move till I call." He stood rigid above them.
His arms extended and fists clenched holding them to
  stillness,
Holding himself; his forehead grooved with bridling
The insane starts and dispersions of his mind. Some
  channel
He had formed for speech: now who could remember
  what course
He had meant to drive the wild horses of speech?
"You straws be quiet!" There were the stars rolling
  enormous
Courses, the unoriented void; the explosive poison in the
  house yonder; sundown; the flurry of the nations,
But that was over: death, death? He heard Onorio
  moaning a vision. He saw Faith Heriot, white fire,
Lean into flame, he cancelled her cry with: "You here,
  you chosen,

Are the opening of love, you are the wedge in the block,
the blast in the quarry, power and fire have come
down to you,
This poor crack of the coast, between the ocean and the
earth, on these bare hills. God walking in you
Goes north and gathers multitude and takes the cities to
give you. What does he require, there is no com-
mandment?
For love, for the broken order of the universe: nothing
but acceptance.
That you *be* your desires, break custom, flame, flame,
Enter freedom."
                    They, that had wished before to leap
and cry out, were silent. A woman cried to him
"I flamed once in my life. I am dead." This was the
woman Myrtle Cartwright who had run to her
lover
Through a storm, the time Onorio had his palms pierced.
Barclay, not pausing for thought, but seeing in his
mind
Rain and thunder on the hills: "You lay under lightning
On the white straw: when your husband had died then
the other
Never wanted you again . . . " He thought "It's my
madness
Makes nonsense in the air." But she, screaming and
turning:
"He knows all I have done and what I have dreamed in
the night!" He astonished with knowledge: "There
is one lover
Brushed off the stars to reach down to you, this one will
never leave you."
"Oh my hair" she cried "is the best part of me,"

[121]

She combed the heap with her hands and shook it on the
    air, then suddenly
Leaped up and down before him like flame. He com-
    manded, "Flame, flame!"
And others were leaping. The first, feeling the breath
Choke in her throat, caught in her hands her clothing
And tore it from the throat to the midriff. When others
Disordered their garments Faith Heriot
Seized hers in her two hands at the neck and rigidly
Undid the hands. She spat on the earth and turned
    down
Toward the house, having refused to be comforted.

XXI

                She came to a point
Whence the house was visible: she was not wicked
    enough
To approach it, carrying a fire that the man had kindled,
Would rage inside the black logs . . .
She saw the rock of Point Sur: she went down to the
    house
For fear of going to the rock.
                She saw from the door,
    Randal
Talking with . . . not Natalia, with April. She
    thought,
"He had me and kept Natalia, he will have this one
And keep Natalia: no German had a bayonet.
Oh he chanced nothing, he stayed with the camp
    women."
She found Natalia on the second stairway; who wearily:
"Grandfather keeps calling me: and Rachel is sick:
I can't be in two places. Where have you been?"
"Looking at the horns. Oh, Rachel sick again?"
    Natalia,
Sharply: "What do you mean by again? She's never
Since the week you came." But Faith: "The great horn
On the hill isn't so pretty as the little ivory
Fellow downstairs, who do you think it's flourished at?
Maruca? No, nor the Chinaman." "I can't hear you,"
Natalia answered.

[123]

In the evening Randal followed
April from the table and said "I hated to come home.
I hate this place, I mean to sell it for a share of the
world.
Your world. How could I know that you would be
here,
Making the place beautiful? When you go, what emp-
tiness."
She heard him saying, but her mind gave him no heed,
She was always, these late days, vague with the day-
dream
About making a weapon in Asia, wakening the nomads,
Or finding freedom in dim Asia, her father
Dying by the blight of some star, she inheriting his
means
To seek freedom in Asia. That the dream was ridicu-
lous
She knew, but she forgot the dream was her brother's
New-made in her mind from keeping memories;
And Randal, not perceiving her mind's distance
But only that her face was wistful like a boy's,
Continued and said: "Even before I went over
The sea and learned something, I knew all the while
There was much better in the world than anything I
knew.
Oh, I've known women." She inclined her head, not
hearing
But "over the sea," that meant escape and release,
"Better than I knew," that meant freedom. He em-
boldened:
"I knew breeding, knew what I'd never seen,
The bright lamp of the mind shine through the face.
It's like a story: to have gone over into hell

[124]

And fought with all the horrible faces of death
And lain among his loathsome pickings
Years, then come home and find my dream in my house.
High-bred, shining with mind, my ideal queen.
You know I am bound, you think I speak like a mad-
man.
You don't know me . . . April . . . I have fighting
spirit,
I was born a fighter, I went because I wanted to: I
fight
For what I want." April perceived
Rather a bodily odor than the spoken words,
And whispered "My mother wants me." The extreme
loathing and fear
Drew not from this man's vanities. He, handling her
arm,
"Oh wait a little. What have I got out of the war?
This uniform and a pistol taken from a prisoner.
I kept the light of ideal love burning in my heart,
I knew there was a girl made for me to worship,
I'd never seen her, tant pis pour moi. But now, now,
I have climbed out of hell and found her."
                                        Faith Heriot crossed over
The end of the room opposite the stair, and taking
Natalia's wrist with one hand pointed with the other.
Natalia gazed and thought of nothing but her child
Sick in the room upstairs, but felt without thought
Like salt in the eyes those two talking: the young sol-
dier,
His handsome trivial face lifted in the shadow,
The lines of the uniform, his back was turned, flaring
From the loins to the straight shoulders; but April's
face
In profile, like a boy's, eager and resolved.

[125]

She had changed, was answering: "You took a weapon
From the enemy? You must be proud of it." "The lit-
    tle automatic
Was all I could smuggle home." "Oh, may I see it?
    My brother,"
She said, "was killed." An old song
Beat her mind like a drum, "Edward, Edward,
Why does your breast—sword was it?—so drip wi'
    blood?
Why does your breast so drip with blood?" He, touch-
    ing her,
"I have it up-stairs." They went up.
                              Natalia
Moved toward the stair thinking that little Rachel
Was sick, needed her mother, but like a dancer Faith
    Heriot
Prevented her and said, "Ah no sweetheart, don't
    follow.
You must endure a little, I endured in the night,
Don't lie to me, when I bit my wrists lying in the bed—
Marks? Oh, yes, look at them—
No wonder the child sickened, what you were doing.
Endure a little." Natalia, the face not changing,
Extended open hands like a blind person,
Touching Faith's breast with finger-tips, the obstacle
Soft and moving, she hardly imagined what obstacle
That blocked her way.
                        At the door up-stairs
Randal thought April would not enter, but she entered,
To see where he kept it. He took it from the drawer,
    blue steel,
Bigger than she'd imagined. Death. She remembered
    the poison

That she had taken from her mother and hidden in the
 car
Among the tools. Randal was saying, "I've only
Five shells to fit the calibre, it's loaded with them.
My old revolver lay in the holster while I was gone
And rusted into a block, the leather draws damp."
"Your hawk's blood was never," it ran in her mind,
"Your hawk's blood was never so red, Edward, Edward."
She looked at Randal, smiling. "It doesn't seem ter-
 rible,
Because I can't imagine it, not really, a man
Killing a man." He put it in the drawer, his head
And hand certainly trembling. "That's clean and easy,"
He answered, "but what burst men to spatters . . .
 April,"
He said clutching her wrists; she writhed herself back-
 ward.
She'd thought the child would be in the room, it was not,
But in the next one; he said "Who's lived years
Between the teeth, takes his joy where he finds it.
Watching them grind his friends: we never counted
To-morrows, to-morrow we were mashed." He knelt
 suddenly
And whimpered, "Wolves it makes us. Oh pure and
 lovely,
How could you know the terrible ferocity of men?
That all your clear, bright beauty, shining with spirit,
Untouched, ideal . . . I can't bear it." He wept in
 his hands;
She, freed, stood gazing. The pistol in the second
 drawer.
This man appointed to outrage the abstraction of her
 mind
With comic attitudes. He said, "I kept my ideals

Bright and clean through it all, I believe in goodness,
In *ro*mance." She left the room and heard Faith Heriot
    down-stairs:
"No, no, but give them time. I give you the long
    nights.
Wait." At the stair-head she met Natalia and felt
Her eyes like rods in the dark: then they were drawn
Home like a snail's. No word; a tension, a violence
Passing, and then Faith's voice in the stair, her laughter.
Natalia went to the child's room and April to her
    mother's.

XXII

Faith mounted two flights, to old Morhead's. She heard
    a rhythmic
Swinging noise in the room before she entered, she
    found him
Swinging his arms—the left one full length, the other
Was lame at the shoulder, he swung it shortened—
So that the nerveless body was shaken on the bed.
She stood in the door, eyeing him for monstrous, in the
    dim lamplight.

She thought nothing, it drew through the mind under
    thought:
Embryo, waiting to be born,
Lying in the house his mother.
When he was young he made his own mother.
Being old he entered her, laid off
All faculties, all will,
To lie passive in the womb.
She has lost the medicine. He flaps in the womb
Like a child flapping in the womb.

"Ah what's the matter grandfather?" He did not hear
Until she spoke shrilly the second time.
The arms kept swinging; a hole in the white beard
Opened and babbled in the earthy voice: "Nothing.
Nothing but the arms to dance with." He let them fall.
"How did you know they're dancing on the hill, I didn't
    tell you?"

She turned the lamp up and saw the shame in his eyes.
"What hill? Uh," he coughed, twitching the arms,
    "who dancing?"
She cast her hands up to the throat of her dress,
Caught hold as if to tear it, her lips tortured
Away from the teeth. The hands relaxed. "A hairy old
    fellow
With a big horn, the women dancing around him.
Up on the hill toward Hayworth's." She saw the arms
    rising.
"Be quiet, little Rachel's sick, grandfather. That
    Barclay,
The same man that was here."
                                    The monstrous fœtus
Beating the walls of the womb.
Nothing can keep it from growing.
Nothing. Fatality. Moons
Up to the tenth have whetted
Their sickles on the rock at Point Sur.
The house shook in the little earthquake
Was the first pain.
It made its mother, her labor is upon her.
How shall I endure the day
Of the monstrous birth-pangs?

"Rachel is sick, we must be quiet, now it's bedtime."
She laid her hand on the arm and when it was quieted
Fished under the bed for the bottle with the wide neck
That lay by the flat pan; she drew the bed-covers
Down to the knees, and bending above the faint
Dry and inhuman odor of the bed drew over to its flank
The flattened body, joined it to the dull glass,
Her spirit raging on the hill, heard the vague rain.

XXIII

The child in the dim light twisted her little features,
Moaned in her sleep, drawing up the knees, and often
Sighing hopelessly, pushed back the coverlet without
    awakening.
Her fever increased. Natalia replaced the coverlet.
Randal opened the door quietly. "She's better?
When are you coming?" She thought of her baby's
Pretty arrogance the days of her health, the pitiful
Self-confidence, nothing could hurt her. "I can't leave
    her,
Randal." The small, tired head twitched over on the
    pillow
The hundredth time, sighing. Randal returned
And lay on his bed. "I used to think of this place
Tenderly, all for Natalia's sake, in the packed entrain-
    ments
That drew toward hell; yes, and in the few hours
Of drunken happiness, remember thinking most tenderly
Of the pure woman to return to, I impure but her sol-
    dier.
And now there's nothing in the house but a sick child."
The old horror of death that might drop down in a mo-
    ment,
And could it be heard coming? returned to forbid
Sleep: the mere phantasy of death excited again
Wrathful desire: risk dropping the unemptied wine-
    cup?

He had rights. He had made sacrifice for her and the
child,
For the future, for their freedom and safety. He rose
And gazed toward April's door down the dark hallway
And turned softly the knob of the other. Natalia
Sat by the bed but certainly the child was quieter.
He embraced her arm with his fingers. "She doesn't
wake up.
She doesn't need you." The trouble in her face angered
him.
"You're troubled about nothing serious." She thought
If she could lead the intolerable whispers
Into the hallway and hide them. She held the latch
To keep it from clicking and attempted to tell him
About Rachel's illness. He thought of death
Comes down like a hawk—on the man. What did
Natalia,
Inexhaustible fountain of life, know of death? He
alone
Menaced in the house, "Come," he said, drawing at her
arm,
Trembling, his habit of fear wearing desire for a wolf-
skin
Not to know its own face. Suddenly her mind
Solved its distraction; in a moment, in white light,
Saw the slant eyes of terror and the thirsting mouth,
And her own motherhood, mother of this changeling also
Who had come to the house like a strange man: even to
Faith Heriot
A sort of mother: they all drained her. Dear, if her
pity
Could yield him peace. It was true the child slept,
this other
Child was unable to sleep.

[132]

Undressing herself
In the next room, smiling wearily, she bared
The breasts before she thought of loosening the skirt.
More prominent and larger than the mould in his mind
They coarsened him with sudden anger and he took
Roughly, and still half clothed, what was about to be
    given,
Raging as over an enemy. Natalia kept patience,
He would rest soon, she could return to her vigil with
    the other.
But Randal imagined April Barclay humbled
By force, the proud and the pure: avenging his felt
Unacknowledged feebleness, dividing desire
Into imaginary violences; the strain-shocked mind
Returning on adolescence.
                    Some psychic remnant
Was it, that frustrate and perverse, wasting
From that incapable passion wandered in the house?
April Barclay, feeling a phantom violence,
Whined in her sleep and felt him—the monstrous
    father—
Hoop the earth with his will, the stars wavered in prison.
The bruise on her cheek awakened her, the hand had
    been clenched
Under the bruise and hurt it. She could not endure
    nightmare,
She got up and began to dress in the darkness.
He possessed all the region. His spirit.
                        It is not possible
A man's spirit possess more than his members; but the
    ocean soul of the world
Has whirlpools in its currents, knots in the tissue,
    ganglia that take

Personality, make temporal souls for themselves: may
   parallel a man's before they are melted. He, fooled,
Counts his great hour, he appears to have broken his
   limits, imposed himself outward. Without subjec-
   tion no Cæsar,
First the subjection. Without form first no phantom.
   I knew that it had a spirit,
This coast of savage hills impendent on the ocean, in-
   secure on the ocean; and few and alien
Humanity reaping it and not loving it, rape and not
   marriage,
Dream a bad edge on the demon. They felt it in the
   night
Take flesh and be man; the man imagined himself God;
   the people were fooled,
Touching reality a little, simply not geared to engage
   reality; the cogs clash and withdraw,
Some impulse was caught, the noise and the spark of
   the steel kissing, a myth and a passion.
                              Barclay had bidden them
Build fires on the hill; they were like happy drunkards
   around the great fires, but Barclay
Entered the hut at nightfall and lay on the blanket.
He heard Onorio Vasquez prophesying and the women
Shout by the fires; he was perfectly convinced and at
   peace.
He awoke in an hour and thought "What shall I do?
The strain, the unendurable strain and deceit. Kill
   myself?"
He lay deprived in the awful return of sane thought,
Not daring to recall his evidences
Nor piece together the hollow miracles . . .
He knew in a flitting instantly forgotten moment

That sanity was too frightful to endure: and murmured
    to himself
"Why do I make pain? Why do I make death? I have
    turned to love men:
All for discovery." His mind unfolded into madness
    and resumed its glory, narrowed to a point
The innumerable stars. "I am also outside the stars,"
    he thought in the wild hush, rising, "the infinite
Nothing outside them, the room . . . room . . . the
    firmament unreason
That has no wings. I do not myself
Know what I am . . . there. In the unconceived, the
    embryo *before* conception." Shaken with his own
Divine mystery, in sacred silence . . . When he came
    outside
A woman arose from the red coals and anxiously
Leaped up and down before him. He answered, "Un-
    happy,
I am in the young men, have you not found me?" She
    answered
"I have kept myself clean till now." "Change. God
    has changed."
She crouched by the coals, wept and would answer
    nothing.
He walked across the scattered people by the dying
    fires,
Feeling the south wind in the stubble of his beard and
    thinking, "I shall never
Sleep any more, I have all my desire." Of those by the
    red fires many were sleeping,
A few lifted to watch him. Down the hill in the dark
He heard murmurs of pleasure, he had commanded them
    to find God in each other; and voices of anger

One way in the dark; by one of the fires the stammering
  of happy drunkards.   They hushed, feeling him
  pass them,
The bottle was hidden.   He angrily: "Nothing is denied
  you.
Why do you want forgetfulness, you are out of the net?
  Yet nothing is denied you."   The woman among
  them, the puckered
Face and shawled head, she stood up swaying like a
  spurt of black fire: "I am old.
Have you changed that?"   He felt the skies of his
  mind
Suddenly be turned and focus upon her, she also felt
  them
And slid to the earth.   He said "I will change it.   When
  I set you
Back of the bleeding womb and *before* conception."

XXIV

Faith Heriot had dreamed that she was buried in the
    earth,
Roofed in with terrible centuries of silent darkness,
On her back, breathless: then a tall tree grew erect
Out of the middle of her body and towered on the soft
    air,
The pride, the enormous girth of the trunk . . . She
    heard old Morhead
Waken and wave his arms in the dark on his bed,
A little at first. She heard a wind gathering
Begin to push at the roof, the wind had wakened him.
The monstrous embryo be born?
The waking nightmare was less endurable, she rose
And found her hands clutching the throat of her night-
    dress.
She unclasped them by force, assuring herself Natalia,
To-night, would never lie down but sit by the child.
Perhaps Rachel was dying, she thought, with bitter
Unconfessed pleasure, now the seasons turned back-
    ward
And nothing remained rational, the mad God on the hill
Possessed the region. His spirit.
                      She felt him on the
    stairs
In the thick dark, she felt him crowding the hallway.
She entered the room they kept the child in. Natalia

Was not in the room, the child was beating the bed with
    its arms
In the lamplight, the eyelids lifted from blanks of fever.
Faith fixed her eyes on the partition, toward the next
    room,
Torturing her hands.
                        Natalia had whispered
Through the dim abstraction of her patience, "Dear
    are you done?
I should go back." He had plowed and not sown, the
    plowshare
Blunted and failed in the furrow "Ah, you slack skin,"
He answered, "who wore you out when I was in hell?
Damn you, go back to him." She answered, "I haven't
    deserved . . .
Randal, I haven't deserved . . ." He, between shame
And obscure terror bending over the bedside,
Took her throat in his nailed fingers, but sparing to stop
    the breath,
"It has to be settled, I'm the master in the house.
Say it, that I'm the master. You know that I loathe
    you,
But while I have to live with you. Say it." She clutch-
    ing
His wrist with her hands, "Rachel is sick, let me go."
"First say it." She was mute, her face changing, and
    her eyes
Warred against his: but Randal's wavered, and Natalia:
"What happened to you to make you a fool and a
    coward,
What did they do to you?" He shuddered and struck
With the free hand, "Ah, that's what you want, what
    you want,"
He loosed the other, "want more?" She rose in the bed,
[138]

Holding her hands before her face, whispering "Now
    I see clearly
That you're the master." She touched the corner of
    her lips
And stared down at the fingers. "Tell me sometime
What they did to you to make you . . . like this." He
    had turned,
She holding up at the waist her remnant clothing,
Went from that room to the other and bent to the child's
    bed
With sharp, quick breath, she had seen Faith Heriot but
    only
As one misery the more. Faith touched her head,
Not for disgust able to touch the bare shoulder,
And said "How horrible you are, you have to have him.
How many times again before morning? Ah, ah,"
The words crumbled in her mouth. Natalia bent lower
Over the child. From Faith the intolerable world
Drained like blood from a wound, life shallowed and
    thinned
Until it seemed a shining and blade-thin pool,
Like a flat moon hardly wetting her foot-soles,
She bloodless spired to a point from and spoke easily
Now it was drained, her purged consciousness
Had hardly a part in the saying, "It is time, dear.
I always loved you, it is time when it grows old and
    dirty,
There are too many people. I would go with you
And help you if you like. I am almost, already."
    Natalia
Saw the child's face ecstatic, blank-eyed,
But the mouth shrivelled and the arms swinging cramped
    arcs
Beyond her understanding, and Faith Heriot: "I think
[139]

She wants to be born, she too.   That fellow's been call-
   ing
All over the world."   Natalia quieted the arms
And bent her cheek to Rachel's.   "You are right to
   hold her," Faith said,
"The first brings enough misery.   More life, more misery.
I have been holding myself.
The thing would be to find out a way of getting *un*born.
I have found out a way."
                           Randal entered the room,
Barefoot, in shirt and trousers, he had heard the trailing
Monotonous voice.   He trembled still.   "A great peace
   to come home to.
Tell it, let me hear."   But Faith Heriot: "Oh wonder-
   ful, again?
All the long night, Natalia."   Natalia not lifted
The cloud of her hair; Randal: "Go up you thin wire.
Dear," he said to Natalia, "I'm sorry.   The nerves go
   bad.
I brought them home crackled: there's something in the
   air.
I came to tell you."   No one answered, and the child
As if disturbed by silence moaned wearily and struggled
   to rise,
Thrusting with the hands.   Natalia sobbed broken voices,
But Faith having her mind fixed on destruction:
"Oh cover her, it's the crazy God calling.
Don't let her be born again for once is bad enough.   I
   tried to crawl home,
I stuck in the cancer.   Listen Natalia,
Let it go in if you have to, never let it come out.   Mouse-
   trap.
I had yours killed," she said to Randal, "my mother
Paid for it.   Oh, I can think of anything.   Your nerves

[140]

Cracked? Mine are wires." He approached her quietly
  and snatched
The thin arm with his hand. "You've got to go up.
You can't play mad here. If you've got to be taken
I'll take you, you've got to be quiet." She laughing
And twisting her lean shoulders, "Oh I'll be your April.
Natalia tell me where you keep the mouse-poison,
He thinks I'm a girl. He ought to know. Randal,
Do you remember the dune under the bushes?
We cheated you though." He drew her to the door.
  Natalia
Stood up, the look of patience had hardened to stone;
The firm breasts and firm flanks, a surface, the eyes even
Were surfaced, though they fixed themselves on the
  others
Were neither giving nor taking. Her giant self-enclosure
Dwarfed the others, all the balance was altered, the
  baby
Under the partial covering struggled on the bed
At the height of her knees little as if newly born.
And Faith at the door, straining to play a part
Under the surfaced eyes, dancing before the divine
Idol: "I made a pitiful boy, good-bye Natalia.
When an old lover takes you by the arm.
Here's the end of play-time, when the man comes women
  stop playing.
Oh you can do as you like." He thrust her outward
And locked the door. He turned inward, but rather
On the room than on Natalia. "Now I've found you out.
It took me two days. Oh well, you change easily
By God I'll see you. Is Rachel better?" She answered
"I've thought of a medicine," she still was erect
In the same standing, but the stone surface and shine
Matted to soft and gray, all the height and majesty

[141]

Nulled, she was like a shadow in the room, all the weight
Disbodied that had seemed dangerous; whatever had
    enforced
The surface now drawn inward or dissolved away.
The child appeared quieter of pain.

XXV

Faith Heriot
Stood by the door, her hands gathered to her throat,
Saw April Barclay come through lamplight, through the
  open doorway
Of Randal's room. She thought "news for Natalia,"
Her mind fixed on destruction, and laughed, "You missed
  him,
He's here with his wife," trembling and laughing, but
  certain
That what she thought of was false, herself was turned
  woman,
April held hidden under the coat something
That men have: "What are you carrying in front of
  you?" She answered like someone
Smiling in the good passage of a mixed dream,
"We'll be good friends," and passed her. Faith followed
  whispering:
"The fellow on the hill, you know him, he calls the
  dances.
What is he making you do?" But April had passed
With a boy's gesture and entered her mother's room,
Shutting the door softly.

XXVI

Randal came out to the hallway
Having heard passages by the door; he saw Faith Heriot
Mount the dim stair, he turned dully to sleep.
He awakened after an hour and some person
Stirred in the room: he lay happily attentive: perhaps
  Faith Heriot . . .
The world has turned strange but April would never.
When he turned over on the bed the fumbling was quiet.
He reached matches and when the motion again
Began its patience, lit one by flicking it on his thumb-
  nail
After a manner he used, and saw Natalia
Still bare to the loins turning from the chest of drawers,
The second drawer was open, she drew out her hand.
He thought she looked for a clean night-dress and had
  missed the drawer.
"Oh make a light, I'm awake." She turned and pushed
  home
That drawer and opened the one above it; the match
Died, and he heard in the darkness the drawers moving
Again, the blind noises of search. He got up
And lighted the lamp. Her eyes appeared lidless
And lacking iris, round vacant ports of a wrecked ship,
So big that the breasts looked little. She said quietly:
"Rachel has died. I have saved . . . she is saved
  everything.

Where does it go to, in the air? I was looking for a
    key . . .
Rachel has died." He cried like a child, "Oh. Oh.
Why did you not call me? Oh! You are lying,
By God," he ran to the next room and the lamp
Shone dimly there. The frightfully little
Blue doll's face on the bed: wet when he touched it,
Like wet putty; he shook his hand, moaning, and made
    more light.
The eyes half open, the nostrils pinched shut, the
    pillow
And the yellow hair darkened with moisture. A gasping
Hysteria like claws in his throat, all the house heard
    him
Controlless, lamenting more his own terror
And the general ruins of the earth.

                    Faith Heriot had
    heard a rasping
Whisper of dry boughs to a coming storm when she went
    up-stairs,
And bent above old Morhead's bed in the darkness,
"What's it now, old friend, not sleeping?" The earthy
    voice:
"Isn't my son enough for her but you must serve too?
Make light for me." She saw by matchlight the covers
Half off the bed, the flattened fork of the body;
By lamplight the hands against the thighs, rubbing them,
The dry and withered; and the earthy voice she had
    never
Heard tremble before was shaken: "They've got new
    feeling.
The pulse prickles. Look," he said, his lean finger
Shook like the compass-needle to a stand, pointing
The gnarled left foot, jointed and sinewed creature

Weak and white from deep sea, that while she watched
    it
Moved painfully, the tendons
Drawn, and the toes and the foot turned on the ankle,
Turned and returned.
                     The air about her head vibrated
    like fire.
The horror of birth: she confused in her mind
The log house with her mother,
In whose womb putrescence
And old disease . . . who had kept the death in her
    womb
To pay the extinction of life
Out of her daughter's.   The monstrous
Lump was ready to be born.
Death was ready to be born
And walk in the world, she thought not consciously, her
    fingers
Flew once more to the throat of her dress and clutched it,
"But I will be unborn and be still in the darkness,
Unbirth, to lie down with death, lie with death . . .
    My father in the lighthouse
Read the bible," she said, "when I was little,
King David was old and couldn't walk they gave him
A young girl for warmth. I'll warm you, in a minute
Death will get up and walk." She lying by his side
Chafed the dry skin on the concave thighs
Tenderly with her hands, because she loved death.
He was like a father, and when she heard Randal crying
Under the floor it was like a dream. She rose up
Vaguely and did not go to the crying but went down
The second stairway, holding the lamp in her hand,
Full of hatred of Natalia. She found her in the kitchen.

"You've done it, have you?"   Who answered coldly, "Not
   yet.
He's hidden it out of its place."   "What?"   "Ah the
   tool,
The tool," but Faith, bewildered, "To think, my God,
I called those slack mounds beautiful!   Get on some
   clothes
Before they take you."   And Natalia: "Who has been
   with you
That your eyes shine . . ."   The man's wailing through
   the open doorways
Covered the words, and Natalia again, her lips
Twisting over the teeth in the smoky lamplight:
"What a fool that is.   Nothing, nothing."   Faith, watch-
   ing
Her right hand folded with some hidden utensil
In the cloth at her groin: "I hate you with all my heart.
I hate you with all my heart.   A killer."   She answered
Patiently: "Though you ought to be patienter with me.
Things you said gave me the thought . . . if I remem-
   ber
What you said, it's no matter.   I am not strong enough
To help you much.   World's too stiff to help others,
Except one's own child.   Own.   You could use it after
   me,
Or find your own."   But Faith approaching her she said
"Stop there.   I should like first . . . "   The servant
   Maruca
Came sloe-eyed from her kennel behind the kitchen,
Mazed at the voices.   Natalia moved by the wall
And stood by the coal stove.   "Stand there Maruca.
I ought to say first . . ."   But Faith: "Why should you
   say
Anything?   I saw him do it.   He had the knife—
[147]

Was it a knife?" "I dropped a towel in the pitcher,
I took it and covered her face." "Oh Maruca," Faith
    said, "Rachel has died.
She was sick in the night and died. Did all we were
    able
And could not save her." Natalia said quietly, "I saw
What she had to grow up to, and she was in pain. We
    have to choose
For a wee helpless child. I'd done her a crime
In the conception, made it as right as I could.
For two minutes of hurt bought her eternal heaven.
There honey, there quietness.
I've not the strength to save anyone else
But only myself." She pressed her left hand
Under the left breast. "Oh, tell Randal
That cornered between the stove and the wall can still
Creep through the mouse-hole." She'd unwound the
    right hand
But Faith at the instant flash leaped for the wrist,
And though it dodged her, breast to breast with Natalia
Closed and constrained. They wrestled, remembering
    their loves,
Groaning, Maruca across their shoulders
Cried like a fishing gull. When they fell, Natalia
Struck her head on the iron stove and was quiet, the little
Paring-knife clinked from her fingers.

                      When her mind
    returned
They had laid her on the bed in her own room, and
    Randal
Talked of a fire on the hill, "the whole hill is burning,
Fools, in this wind. They've fired the hill I must go.
My God is there no end?" For the poor remnant
Of the farm stock were fenced on the hill. The women
Heard him crying by the stables, toward the dark dawn.

XXVII

The south wind that in better winters blows rain on
    men's fields
This year blew fire, it rose in the night and snatched the
    embers of the fires
Across the sleeping people, it sowed them in the dry
    grass. The few that watched were not there, for
    Barclay
Had walked in the night southward the ridge, full of his
    exultations; a few followed him; Onorio
Vasquez the vision-seer was at his arm when he stum-
    bled, Myrtle Cartwright was with him; three others
Followed, and all deranged with ecstasy but one with
    whiskey. Barclay, the stars forming and dying
In the measurelessness of his lost mind, stood on the
    hill's brow over Morhead's farmhouse and saw
Lights change in the little windows far down; and he
    saw
The great light glowing and lapsing on the rock of
    Point Sur, in the ocean loneliness; and the sea stars
Brighten and go out through the small cloud-scud, the
    wind increasing. "I am God: but I am secret:"
    and he said:
"You are atoms of humanity and all humanity
A cell of my body: listen, I have turned all my light-
    nings of consciousness

[149]

On the one cell; I have turned to love men. I lift a
    handful from the ocean. What do you see in this
    house,
Onorio, the lights change in the windows?" "The age
    of the world," he stammered, "the new world, power
    is turned backward.
They love pleasure and death." Then Barclay: "I pour
    my life into these bottles, that burst and the life
Spills on the ground, it is inexhaustible, I am the foun-
    tain." The drunkard swaying in the darkness,
    "Elijah
Pop out the cork, clock clock," plopping his thumb
From the sucked cheek; and Onorio Vasquez: "Master
    they prophesy the last days, they are drunk with
    confusion,
What people are these, the women make themselves men
    and the men are unable, the man plows and no seed,
Dreaming of the next field." Then Barclay answered
    "These are the people.
The times they command fate to serve them, then I lay
    waste their fountain. The useless function runs mad
Until power dies. Powers increase and power dies."
    The drunkard fell prone before him,
Having essayed to dance in the wind, tripped up by the
    earthling blackberry vines that trailed on the hill's
    brow,
And Vasquez cried out "No hope, see-saw forever?"
    He answered "Cæsar is not born but the power
    perishes,
The life moves to the skin." And the drunkard: "Be-
    cause I kissed my mother
I have thorns in my skin, Oh that she doesn't love me"
    he wept; and Vasquez: "Be quiet will you, I am
    asking

My lord is there any hope?" Barclay feeling the stars
Turn in his mind: "I have turned to love men. What
    does hope mean, ask nothing foolishly, I take my
    remnant.
I have not done this before, not for the crown of the
    stars: you are out of the net." And he cried
    suddenly:
"To-night my love for whom I turned to love men, the
    bride and the equal-minded, whom I took like a
    tower
Taken by violence, the supreme sacrifice, the lamb of
    God
That bled," he said shuddering, "secretly, that moaned
    for love in the high darkness, the spirit of splendor
Through whom the dark earth blinds Arcturus comes up
    to me: Onorio,
The light of the footprints, the flute-music of the fright-
    ened breathing." He shook like a tall pine, and
    the wind
Began to rage up hill in the darkness.

                                        The wind glided
        from southward
In gusts, like a knife drawn against a whetstone, that
    glides and gives over, so the great wind lay gustily
On the ocean, on the dark rocks of the shore, on the
    secret hills, pausing and thrusting. It gathered the
    embers
Of Barclay's fires among his company to sow them
In grass gemless of dew that long had forgotten
Rain and the green; the white fibers of the hill whis-
    pered to each other: "A holy spirit has come down
To one us with the God that we came from. Have
    courage," they cried, writhing like terror, "we were
    dead already."

The wind slackened, they erected themselves and trembled.

Under the third gathering of wind
Randal Morhead began to cry out through the log house
    over the child that was dead: then April,
Who had sat without moving near the bed of her mother,
    holding the small engine of death
As it were a precious appendage of her own body . . .
    Natalia
Had sought it in vain, April had heard the secret
Comings and goings in the dense house, and suddenly
The man's voice in the bright hysteria wailing like a
    woman's . . . "Mother,
Get up and dress, it is time." She lighted the lamp.
"I have planned everything." When Audis Barclay
Sat up in the bed trembling, with useless questions,
April patiently: "Unless you come I must leave you.
Nobody here will hurt you . . . lock it behind me,
Lie still till morning." She hastily got up: then April
Averted her eyes, feeling not thinking herself
Boy-sexed in the woman's room, and with vague shame
And vague disgust stiffened by the window, her back
Turned on the woman dressing. She watched from the
    window
The lighthouse lighten and darken through the gross
    darkness on the rock of Point Sur,
She heard the womanish voice of lamentation
Lift and pause in the house. She cried "Are you ready?"
And swept her mother uselessly questioning
Out of the room by mere impetus of mind
To the stair-head and the turn of the stair and the door;
Then Audis would not go out; but April: "Come mother,
You have come this far. Death is up-stairs, I don't know
    who dead,

[152]

But not innocently, and there's more," she said pointing
Through the open doors to the far room.   Faith Heriot
Came first, her thin back toward them, and Maruca be-
     hind her,
Carrying a third; Faith had the bare shoulders,
Maruca the knees, there was blood in the hair.   Then
     April:
"Oh easily.   Come.   Here's only the wake of that ship
That wills horror on the hill.   I'm going up, mother,
Against the stem and cutwater and change him.   Un-
     happy April . . .
These things are not our miseries but unhappy April . . .
Had a sweet name."   She drew the door open, the storm
Strained through the hollow of the house, the lamp be-
     hind them
Streamed up into death.   She holding Audis erect,
Who bowed over the threshold in the rushing darkness,
Drew her through and drew the door home.   "The elec-
     tric torch,
Wait mother, in the pocket of my coat: I've something
In the hand: reach it."

XXVIII

Barclay cried on the hill, "Where does my love linger?"
A moment the mill-race of the swirling galaxy parted in
    his mind, he saw through an island of peace
That who came up to find him would go to the fires to
    find him, how could one find another on the hill,
Even God on the dark hill? He turned quickly to go
    back to the fires, but Vasquez:
"What are they doing," unable to fetch his eyes from
    the farmhouse windows
Down the headlong wind, "killing their hope, one vessel
    they had made
To swim up time, one little quiverful
Of slender arrows to shoot the future: they have broken
The arrow-shafts in the bundle, what will stand up
    now?" Then Barclay: "Out of *me*
Destruction, out of me renewal, I preserve nothing:
    exult with me.
I take my chosen, I never said I would salvage you all
Out of the net of change and renewal: they climb out
    of the pit to the brink and suddenly they slay
The next step with their hands: I laugh in tempests over
    their heads in the air, and exult, and raise up
The old violence, the old mysticism, the old terror among
    them,
The resurrection of time among them." Myrtle Cart-
    wright

To Vasquez: "Is the old man still living that lies like death
Under the roof?" He with fixed eyes not answered, but Barclay:
"It is time: I called him. Come quickly." They went to the fires,
The far hill like a burning mountain.

                                        Audis Barclay
Sobbed on the dark slope "Has the father's madness
Burst out in the daughter? I cannot go up any farther,
April, April." Who answered "You are talking to the dead.
Now I can neither leave you here nor go back
It's likely I'll have to tell you . . . I'll have to . . .
That I mean patience. I had a sick thought
That looked red at the end but that's over. Use the torch, mother.
Come this way from the bush, now's easier walking.
He . . . April . . ." She panted for breath. "Insane.
A red curtain hung over his mind . . . what beasts in the newspaper . . .
But this you must remember was her own father,
In whom she had natural confidence.
She fought hard, was betrayed by her own . . . soul . . .
Weakness of body." She cried against her mother's silence
"There was a bruise if you'll remember on the cheek!
That you saw. And others. He struck with the fists."
        Audis,
Retractile and sad all her pale years, felt sudden
Calmness and power. "If this were the truth, April."
Who answered "But you can see plainly it was not possible

To live the rest. It would be conceivable, if life
Had been too obstinate in her it might have nour-
      ished . . . succession . . . nature
Goes very blindly. I keep locks on myself
To speak coldly of things in their nature unspeakable.
Because our nerves are like . . . wires in this wind
And have to be kept muted." "What do you mean to
      do?"
"It is not much higher though now so steep, mother.
And I feel perfectly sure of finding him here
On the next brow, and alone or nearly: that was my
      hurry:
We'll find him alone we can speak quietly
And use reason at the least, if possible: we couldn't
      hope to
There by the fires among the fooled people.
Having passed under death if that's a true dream
Cools me. I'd have been hastier. Dear mother,
If there's time afterwards . . . do you hear nothing at
      all
Known in my voice, mother? I cannot
Myself believe, though I remember the pain,
And then the faintness, of death: and the long homesick
      wandering:
That his terrible happiness has flowered
Out of my sister's misery: I Edward your son,
I died in France, hear your real voice and again
Touch you with living hands. *Living* is nothing
To make joy over. . . . It is really no matter
Whether you believe me or not, I have this gladness
Against this horror. . . . Would I dare to go up and
      face him
If I were that victim, mother, that stricken April?
I go coldly, having gone under death;

Nothing of vengeance although I loved her. . . . My
     aim
To bring him down and lay him under restraint
Quietly: I'm armed: you can't run to the law
In the infamous case: nothing but private recourse:
Even if the man were a stranger."
                              Audis stood, saying
"I have always been weak. . . . Oh this delusion," she
     thought,
"Of the strength that might have saved us come back
     to be alive:
She has courage from this. He's with God. Is it de-
     lusion?"
Feeling the strength draw from it. "Dear I have only
A measure of power: I must hold sane: it leaves me
The judge in the world. Armed, you said? Show me."
     She answered,
"I stole a pistol in the house." She folded the cloak
Over her hand, she could not for shame make naked
The vital instrument and symbol of power
To another sex though her own mother. The hard
Hot grip burned in her hand. "I will not go up
Until you show me." "Then, mother," she answered
     swaying
With the great gusts of love warring on shame.
She held it bare in her hand, the sacramental
Exhibition, the awful witness of power.

XXIX

But Audis snatched for it.   April caught back the hand
And the emblem, and shaking with white anger: "I have
    lucky parents.
Feel your own way."   She climbed up the last slope
And on the brow the blackness of the night, the solitude,
    the straining
Wind, were alone.   She stood astonished.   "Not here?"
His dreadful and divine presence was yet so palpably
Covering the hill.   Was it love . . . so impudently
    longed for his presence . . .
"Then it needs killing, good-bye to reasonableness,
There's no escape but hold it straight-pointing, press
    here,
The little steel spring in the handle as he taught me,
Pull this one . . . what else did I fetch it up for?
Go on to the fire and find him."   She had stood, and now
    heard
A voice from the earth, her mother's fallen to the earth
On the hilltop near her feet and thrusting a voice
Like a torn stalk up into the wind: "Ah dearie,
If ever it's fired fling it away, fling it away,
They couldn't trace it to you, not bought nor given.
Wait for me dear."   She ran from the voice toward the
    fires,
The hillside over the saddle sheeted with fires,
And still heard crying: "April!" but afterwards, "Ed-
    ward . . ."

[158]

That touched her, she turned and waited. "I am in the
wave, mother,"
She thought to herself, "runs from the know-nothing
ocean.
I feel it drawing and thrusting me up: all that I think
Or feel's less than the foam." She choked with fear.
"Doing has no thread to thinking, nobody knows
What's made in the dark water till it pops the surface."
The gliding earth-moon, the electric circle of the torch
Turned down for timid footing crept nearer. "Can I
stand all night?"

In the house under the hillside Natalia
Rolled her head on the mats of her black hair, saying,
"It's early to dance. No, you must leave me to-day,
I've got a headache." Faith Heriot stared at the face,
That wore through its pain so wonderful a look of wan-
tonness,
The slack lip and the teeth, the half-closure of the eyes,
And seeing the blood was oozing again through the black
hair
She said, "Maruca, get more water in the pitcher."
Who having gone down to fetch it came back trembling,
The pitcher empty in her hand. Meanwhile Faith Heriot
Had carried the wash-bowl with its ruddy water
And the dark clots at the bottom, to the window to
empty.
She leaned from the window and saw the red sky stream-
ing
Over the hill like dawn in the wrong quarter,
And heard what she supposed was the surf running
Under the distant rock of the lighthouse, it sounded
Like horses running. She turned, and Maruca

Stood trembling with the empty pitcher, the broad gray
 face
Lined with white streaks. "Well, what's the matter?"
 Who answered
That the big table in the dining-room had been thrown
 over
And the picture of a sail-ship on the wall was dancing,
"I came up-stairs then." Faith took the pitcher and
 went down,
And passing the overthrown table thought it was strange
That neither of the dogs had barked all night, not even
 when Randal
Went screaming toward the stable. She drew the water
And went up with the pitcher. Maruca placed the bowl,
Natalia rolled her head on the mats of black hair,
But when the wash-cloth wetted her face Natalia
Instantly ceased to breathe and fluttered both hands,
Making a coarse noise in the throat, but still
Not breathing, and the lips blued. Faith dropped the
 wash-cloth,
Thrust hands under the shoulders and dragged up the
 body,
It would not breathe, she slapped the nipples of the
 breasts,
Then it bowed over and caught breath, and Natalia
Rose from the bed like a snapped-wing hawk that flops
 up
On the sound wing against the children tormenting it
And strikes this way and that way quicker than sight
With beak and talons, so that it seems not to have struck
Yet the hands and the cheeks are bleeding: then the
 snapped wing
Betrays it and it falls but the children are scattered:
She falling back on the bed had not the hawk's look

Nor silence, but chattered inarticulate terror,
And Faith sullenly: "I only wanted to wash
The blood out of your hair." She chattered, "I know
    these towels
With all the drowning ocean in them.
What blood, there was no blood, Oh you white liar
She died by herself." Faith said "There's nothing to
    be afraid of.
Lie still till morning, will you?"
                                    But speaking, her lips
Twitched, and their pallor increased to her cheeks' white-
    ness:
The while Maruca tilted up the black beads
Between the folds of brow and cheek-bones and said
    smiling
"Old grandfather: he got up?" For the boards groaned
Over their heads, a noise of slow shuffling
Motion, and then like a load dragged on the floor
Under the roof. In Faith's mind
The womb's throes in waves
Of animal contraction
Thrust their object: she felt in her mind
Not the knives and grinding
Of the pain she'd never experienced, but sick thrust . . .
    thrust . . .
Complicating with stifling
Drunken abysses of remembered ether;
She felt the rings of flesh
Drawing and sucking
In waves on the bearded load, he had made his mother,
And she heard Natalia, who perceived nothing: "Oh no,
I did quiet her, the man on the hill called her,
She was too sick to dance I wanted to quiet her,

And I'd have fixed myself and Randal but he hid the
    gun,
We've got to go up." Faith from the sick vertigo
Gathering her native courage like a hand plucking
A dropped coin from a swirl of deep water: *"I've* got
    to go up.
But you lie quiet." But while she spoke slow foot-
    steps
Hung halt on the dull stairway, from tread to tread
Dropping, and the hand-rail creaked in the dark. The
    door of the room
Was open, they could hear clearly. It stopped at the
    stair foot
While one breathed twice, then drew down the dark
    corridor,
And now he was heard breathing. He rested on the
    door-knob
Of the next room. Natalia rose naked from bed
As if she'd been awaiting him, and in the doorway:
"Go in, grandfather. Grandfather look at Rachel.
She had a wound that would have poisoned her," she
    said,
"What all our misery comes out of." But Faith behind
Caught her by the arms above the elbows and jerked her
Sidelong against the bed, "Get cloth around you,
You dough-image, this sort of game's finished.
We sailed up wind of the flesh before you were sleeping,
And near the fires. She's been asleep, Lazarus,
And hasn't heard the world change. Where are you
    going?"
He answered calmly in the earthy voice: "The little
    one's dead.
I heard my son. Keep the quiet while I look at her."
He entered the dim room, the lamp had burned dim,

Faith cried behind him, "What quiet? There's none in
    the place.
They tip the tables over and dance the pictures,
And they'll have picked her out of the bed and hung her
    in the air
Shining: the quiet." But he sat where his son
Had sat crying by the bedside, and very gravely
Gazed at the face, the small gray and deformed
Features in the dim gold frame of the hair. Natalia
Entered the room, she had somewhat covered herself,
Maruca helping; but Faith stood by the door,
Her hands pressed on her thighs, visibly shaking,
Thrusting with the chin and the lean throat. Old Mor-
    head
Said very gravely: "It is a pity. Good child.
Though all its playtime's over it was saved something.
We'll take it up with us." Natalia leaned over him
With insane picking fingers, twitched back the covers,
Slid up the linen to the breast of the little body,
"See here, see here grandfather, I had good reason.
She had a wound, do you see, in the eye of the body,
When they grow up it turns a running ulcer
And all that have it are unhappy." He answered with
    patience,
Not restraining the crazy hands, "What you suffer,
    Natalia,
Though two are worse than one for a woman, would
    seem
A very little toward the end. I have studied suffering
While I was dead up in the air, and before,
When I lived free: I have studied life and I find
Nothing ever very terrible. But now we've been called?"
Natalia pushing him with her shoulder leaned low
Over the bed and saw and smelled the wet stain

Under the little thighs, the bladder had emptied
In the struggle at death: the odor and the stain pierced
Like spears through her veiled brain, the child's dear
    babyhood,
Her own awed care and love remembered came flooding
Back on the broken mind and she flung herself
Like water on the dead, her wordless and wild crying
Like flesh torture-disjointed. Faith Heriot looked in
And called through it, "Take off your hand Lazarus.
No fondling, we have nothing to do with each other, we
    are all turned up
Like needles to the north to the black maypole
Stands on the mountain." He rose trembling, she saw
The waggle of the white beard against the dark lamp-
    light,
And the drained eyes. As much as his were drained out
Hers filled with power, and her throat. "Come on old
    scarecrow,
Born at the wrong end of the horn, old baby,
You know what you were brought out for. And you
    Natalia,
I loved you once: but at the vile end, when it sticks,
Then we must turn to God. Take Rachel up to him,
He'll make it live, this old Lazarus was dead
Two or three years and look at him." Natalia looked
    up:
"Is he good, grandfather?" He answered groaning, "No
    matter.
Starving people can't ask. Dawn's here." Faith Heriot
Exulted and cried: "He calls the dances, he is the
    column,
Come up to the stone on the hill. He is what women
And drained old men want in their dreams,
What the empty bodies howl for. I made a false one,

And look at the woman!" Natalia stood up and said
With hollowed eyes across the twilights, the doubled
And mixed, the gray window and the murk lamp:
"I wish that the air were sudden poison, and the sun
Blind, and the black sea piled over the mountains.
I wish the wind that roars on the shaking glass
Were a sword in our throats. They ought to have it cut
    off them
When they're born, we'd be quieter. I wish that the rock
Would spit and vomit, fountains of twisted fire
Catch the spirit with the life: that everything moving
Or feeling between the stars and the center were silent.
That every baby in the world were like this baby.
Take me to the God." Old Morhead, his face like scrib-
    bled paper
With three round holes burnt through it, leaned over
    on the bed,
On the head-boards of the bed, his left leg suddenly
Failing under him: he seemed to pray and it straight-
    ened,
And he said, "We need saving." But Faith to Natalia,
Who stooped and gathered to her breast the dead child:
"I don't know you. I don't know what you are.
We're going to the hill. I've learned what *I* am."
    Maruca
Helped Natalia on the stairs; Faith helped old Mor-
    head.

XXX

Back in the heart of the seamed mountain of the night
    Barclay
Returned to his awakened people. Some of the people
Were huddled in groups without a center, having no
    power to look to; others gathered their gear
Hastily, in fear the flame creep windward; a few ran on
    the mountain beating the fainter fire-lines
With broken branches, crying to each other through the
    red smoke in vain. Barclay leaped up to a broken
Farm-wagon on the bare hill, crying, "I am all these
    things: I am the storm and the fire:
What ailed you to scatter? Because I was not here at
    your head? I was here at your head.
You blind saw but the fires and did not know me, you
    deaf heard but the wind, you ape-descended
Unable to see God but clothed in the contemptible body
    of the ape. I will take you and open you,
And when you see power you will know me, when you
    see peace, or beat your hands on the quietness of
    rock,
Me, the one power. Let it burn. How could I be God
But be the dregs of contempt, the uneasy slime under
    the glory, be you, you navelled sicknesses
That shiver in the wind: as well as the glory: as well
    as the sacred flesh and spirit that panting

Adorable terror, the young bride and not a maiden to the
    bridegroom waiting, the very daughter to the father,
Not virgin of him: I am God and the laws are mine and
    the times mine: comes up on the hill, the incarnate
And perfect April of the world, the shining
Foil for the love."
                     April stood under him and heard
    her own name
Sail on the storm: her teeth grated together and she
    saw in her mind
A naked white degrading image of herself
Spread out on the storm like a four-pointed star
Twirl down his torrent publicly: she turned on her
    mother,
And her words had no breath in them and fell like
    sparrows
In the battering wind, but Audis answered, and April:
"You still think that I'm April. Oh mother
April is dead. *I* paddled up out of darkness.
I know death. As for April she'll be safe though I send
    him.
The dead have nothing to do with each other, they're
    turned
Like needles to the north to the black maypole . . ."
    She worked inward
Among the packed bodies. He stood culprit for all the
    streaming
Shadows of time: Oh with the small steel tool—the
    power without reason or pity, rogue elephant
Bayed on the world's end fires . . .
                     Barclay looked down
And saw the mask of her face lit by the fires.
The loins and shoulders parted out of her path;

She stood in the ring of people, the horror of his love
Came down from the height.
On the fire-lit side of the
world Onorio Vasquez
With his eyes like desert caves dreamed atonement: the
people
Never could make peace with God:
The son of man has gone up, the God of might has
come down:
Onorio Vasquez has seen in all his visions
Not one relative to life, not one within light-years
Parallel to the nature of things, and the peace in his
eyes
Is like the sun shining from desert caverns.
"Now I can see what all the cruelty was for,
And why the stars were not blackened when they saw
the people.
The giant Christ that brought fire to his tribe, he sneaked
it from heaven
And hung on the mountain pierced with splinters of
rock;
The Christ that brought us love and was punished on
the tree
With piercing iron: he has come from the cave fortress,
from the trees of the forest,
He has risen like a comet streaming blood and bitter-
ness for splendor,
Man has flung down the sword, God has ungated the
garden,"
He cried with his face black against the red. "But I
have been virgin
All night though God commanded me to take a woman.
I saved myself virgin for the sake of my visions."

Myrtle Cartwright,
On the dark side of the world, her face fire-brightened,
Her eyes like red stones in the firelight: "What is the
     white light
Flutters four wings in the sky, lightens from four eyes?
The double-crested wonder, the double-throated,
The marriage of white falcons in the height of the air,
Here falls a feather as white as anguish.
The daughter of man has flown from the small planet
To be mated with God, here's a dropped flamelet.
She is crucified in the air with kisses for nails
Lining the palms and foot-soles, and the lance of delight,
The dear agony of women . . ."
                    April Barclay
Heard no one crying, she saw the dark mountain come
     down, she held her soul's life
Under the storm of the cloak; the steel savior, the life
     of the male spirit of her body; knowing clearly
That if she stumbled into the pit of womanhood there
     was no living.
"I am Edward, father, I have come." "My dream on
     the mountain," he answered, "you act nothing but
     echoes me." She knew then
That the young man would desire to kill his father
And never could do it. The vault of the skies of her
     mind
Fell into fragments, through the streaming ruin she
     heard the scream of her mother: that was the
     signal
Of the act accomplished: both-sexed can love inward,
She turned the love inward, between the small breasts,
Under the cloak, planted fire easily, fired twice
Falling. But after the shock, lying on the earth
                    [169]

With mind wasting at peace, feeling one thing done
  wisely
In the vast insanity of things . . .

Barclay bent over
  her
And opened the cloak; the body was there but not
  April; he smelled the gun's breath and lifted his
  face
Into abstract existence; consciousness abstracted from
  feeling; the wires of pain-pleasure
Burned out, the ways of consciousness cleared perfectly.
Himself was the desert that he had entered; these mil-
  lions of millions
Were grains of sand of himself, all present, all counted,
All known. The thing can hardly be spoken further.
  April was dead:
But all that passion a fable: had served the purpose.
The dead have ears but no mouths, one's like another.
They are grains of sand on the sand; the living are
  grains of sand on the wind; the wind crying "I
  want nothing,"
Neither hot nor cold, raging across the sands, not shift-
  ing a point,
Wanting *nothing:* annihilation's impossible, the dead
  have none: it wants, actively, *nothing:*
Annihilation's impossible, the dead have none. "I am
  the desert.

You living
That worry over this dead, this is the lamb of sacrifice,
  why do I do these things?
Let each one take a rope of the hair for long remem-
  brance, and then be silent. Dawn has come in.
It is not as if the matter were important. Oh, if the
  old woman . . .

Audis I got two children on you in spite of you before
     I was God: where are your children?
You had poison hidden, you were not selfish with it, you
        fed it to the children . . . not soon enough, mostly
They catch them in the act under Mount Venus.   Anni-
     hilation's impossible, the unborn have none."

XXXI

                              Faith Heriot had come,
And said "The old man fell down after all. Oh here's
      another one, here's another, Natalia." And Bar-
      clay:
"Why should you riot over the child, hack her in pieces,
For each a mouthful." And wearily: "I will gather my
      desert dust over my shoulders. Being God must
      go on.
I never turn to love them but out the blood spurts.
Come north with me, I will tell you what it is to be
      God. North on the cities: go along with my wind
And shepherd my devouring fire."
                                Audis rose from
      the body of April
And stood with eyes like stab-wounds but with fawning
      shoulders,
Giving him what she had found in the cloak. "It is not
      empty.
I am clean in this matter." He laughed and took it,
      saying "Look behind you." She thought
That when her head was turned he would give her in-
      stant
Deliverance, and then himself. She turned and stood
      waiting,
But fell in a moment, and had not seen Natalia,
Yielding the child out of her arms to a woman

Who thought that the child slept, stoop at the guardless
Body of April, and saying "Randal he told me
She has eyes in both the breasts," tear the light clothing
From the breast down to the belly, call the wounds eyes,
And beat the flesh with her hands. Faith Heriot cried
    out
"Oh yes it is time," and tore her own at the throat,
Feeling the pleasure all night refused fly through her
    body
Like fire eating white grass.
                    But Maruca: "You never
    tamed me,
The mountain-lion under the thick slow body,
The long cat of the woods: you made me serve in the
    kitchen.
God came secretly and gave me a child in my womb,
The Christ of the lions, for whom I shall kill fawns
And feed him on the young of the mountains." She fled
    from the rest,
And cried from the oaks over the rock against dawn
The cougar's cry, and said "He has turned to love lions,
We are wise to the catnipped baits and strychnine, we
    shall hunt men
After the kitten is grown."
                    None heard her; and Bar-
    clay
Passed from among the centered madness over dead
    April; he had dropped the pistol
Among the bacchanal feet; Myrtle Cartwright followed
    him, Vasquez remained; but after a little
Vasquez and certain of the others followed also, but
    like shells moving,
Having shed their spirits over the girl's body in the
    madness at dawn.

Barclay went down to the embers
Of the oak fires, the coals yet glowing; the flame
Roared on the mountains northward. He gathered up
in his hands a heap of red coals. "Never believe
That God sitting aloof inflicts on other flesh than his
own experience and wounds. But at length
I grow weary of discovery." He spilled the fire on the
earth and struck his hands together, then fragments
Of blackened flesh fell from the palms. "My strength's
not tapped yet. But now I remember when the
earth was innocent,
Before this heresy life celled the slime. Clean rock
Suffers no wrong. But even in the ages of the beasts,
before I brought down
These tree-dwellers and made them like little towers
walking, and sphered the brain-vault
To a bubble of fire: there was no cruelty, no traps, the
suffering
Was tolerable. Heautontimoroumenos repents." He
went northward
Across the blackened waste of the hill; who followed him
Ran with the feet ahead of the body, leaning backward
Against the wind's drive.
                         A string of scorched cattle
Ran down toward the ocean, crossing his path. He an-
swered them,
"Eat flesh, I have burnt the pasture. The flesh-eater's
The only honesty, pays cash, peace for a piece.
Learn to quarter your butchers."
                         The wind tumbled
him, he fell on his hands,
The burnt palms cracked and blood ran down from the
fingers.
He stood until they came up to him, the few

That still followed across the black hill. He had passed
    his hand over his brow, the short-bearded face
Was blood and ashes, they saw it without amazement.
    "Pain's," he said, "the foundation. I have turned
    to love men.
I have gathered the souls already, you've not a soul
    among you. Automatisms and gusts of the nerves
Plague you, but think on the nothing
Outside the stars, the other shore of me, there's peace.
I'll save the beasts, too."

                        He ran northward, his fol-
    lowers
Tired and fell off. He alone, like a burnt pillar
Smeared with the blood of sacrifice passed across the
    black hills,
And then the gray ones, the fire had stopped at a valley.
He came to the road and followed it, the waste vitality
Would not be spent. When the sun stood westward he
    turned
Away from the light and entered Mal Paso Canyon.
At the head of the steep cleft men had mined coal
Half a century before; acres of dry thistles
Covered the place where men had labored, and Barclay
Lay down in the mouth of the black pit. After three
    days,
Having not tasted water, he was dying and he said:
"I want creation. The wind over the desert
Has turned and I will build again all that's gone down.
I am inexhaustible."

OTHER POEMS

THE HURT HAWK

The broken pillar of the wing jags from the clotted
    shoulder,
The wing trails like a banner in defeat,
No more to use the sky forever but live with famine
And pain a few days: cat nor coyote
Will shorten the week of waiting for death, there is
    game without talons.
He stands under the oak-bush and waits
The lame feet of salvation; at night he remembers
    freedom
And flies in a dream, the dawns ruin it.
He is strong and pain is worse to the strong, incapacity
    is worse.
The curs of the day come and torment him
At distance, no power but death the redeemer will
    humble that head,
The intrepid readiness, the terrible eyes.
The wild God of the world is sometimes merciful to those
That ask mercy, not aften to the arrogant.
You do not know him, you communal people, or you
    have forgotten him;
Intemperate and savage, the hawk remembers him;
Beautiful and wild, the hawks, and men that are dying,
    remember him.

NOTE ON "THE WOMEN AT POINT SUR"

I

When I considered it too closely, when I wore it like an
 element and smelt it like water,
Life is become less lovely, the net nearer than the skin, a
 little troublesome, a little terrible.

I pledged myself awhile ago not to seek refuge, neither
 in death nor in a walled garden,
In lies nor gated loyalties, nor in the gates of contempt,
 that easily lock the world out of doors.

Here on the rock it is great and beautiful, here on the
 foam-wet granite sea-fang it is easy to praise
Life and water and the shining stones: but whose cattle
 are the herds of the people that one should love
 them?

If they were yours, then you might take a cattle-
 breeder's delight in the herds of the future. Not
 yours.
Where the power ends let love, before it sours to
 jealousy. Leave the joys of government to Caesar.

Who is born when the world wanes, when the brave soul
 of the world falls on decay in the flesh increasing
Comes one with a great level mind, sufficient vision,
 sufficient blindness, and clemency for love.

This is the breath of rottenness I smelt; from the world
 waiting, stalled between storms, decaying a little,

Bitterly afraid to be hurt, but knowing it cannot draw
the savior Caesar but out of the blood-bath.

The apes of Christ lift up their hands to praise love:
but wisdom without love is the present savior.
Power without hatred, mind like a many-bladed machine
subduing the world with deep indifference.

The apes of Christ itch for a sickness they have never
known; words and the little envies will hardly
Measure against that blinding fire behind the tragic eyes
they have never dared to confront.

II

Point Lobos lies over the hollowed water like a humped
whale swimming to shoal; Point Lobos
Was wounded with that fire; the hills at Point Sur en-
dured it; the palace at Thebes; the hill Calvary.

Out of incestuous love power and then ruin. A man
forcing the imaginations of men,
Possessing with love and power the people: a man
defiling his own household with impious desire.

King Oedipus reeling blinded from the palace doorway,
red tears pouring from the torn pits
Under the forehead; and the young Jew writhing on the
domed hill in the earthquake, against the eclipse

Frightfully uplifted for having turned inward to love
the people:—that root was so sweet Oh, dreadful
agonist?—
I saw the same pierced feet, that walked in the same
crime to its expiation; I heard the same cry.

A bad mountain to build your world on. Am I another
keeper of the people, that on my own shore,

On the gray rock, by the grooved mass of the ocean, the
sicknesses I left behind concern me?

Here where the surf has come incredible ways out of
the splendid west, over the deeps
Light nor life sounds forever; here where enormous sun-
downs flower and burn through color to quietness;

Then the ecstasy of the stars is present? As for the
people, I have found my rock, let them find theirs.
Let them lie down at Caesar's feet and be saved; and he
in his time reap their daggers of gratitude.

III

Yet I am the one made pledges against the refuge con-
tempt, that easily locks the world out of doors.
This people as much as the sea-granite is part of the
God from whom I desire not to be fugitive.

I see them: they are always crying. The shored Pacific
makes perpetual music, and the stone mountains
Their music of silence, the stars blow long pipings of
light: the people are always crying in their hearts.

One need not pity; certainly one must not love. But
who has seen peace, if he should tell them where
peace
Lives in the world . . . they would be powerless to
understand; and he is not willing to be reinvolved.

IV

How should one caught in the stone of his own person
dare tell the people anything but relative to that?
But if a man could hold in his mind all the conditions at
once, of man and woman, of civilized

And barbarous, of sick and well, of happy and under
　　torture, of living and dead, of human and not
Human, and dimly all the human future:—what should
　　persuade him to speak? And what could his words
　　change?

The mountain ahead of the world is not forming but
　　fixed. But the man's words would be fixed also,
Part of that mountain, under equal compulsion; under
　　the same present compulsion in the iron consistency.

And nobody sees good or evil but out of a brain a
　　hundred centuries quieted, some desert
Prophet's, a man humped like a camel, gone mad be-
　　tween the mud-walled village and the mountain
　　sepulchres.

V

Broad wagons before sunrise bring food into the city
　　from the open farms, and the people are fed.
They import and they consume reality. Before sunrise a
　　hawk in the desert made them their thoughts.

VI

Here is an anxious people, rank with suppressed blood-
　　thirstiness. Among the mild and unwarlike
Gautama needed but live greatly and be heard, Confucius
　　needed but live greatly and be heard.

This people has not outgrown blood-sacrifice, one must
　　writhe on the high cross to catch at their memories;
The price is known. I have quieted love; for love of the
　　people I would not do it. For power I would do it.

[183]

—But that stands against reason: what is power to a
    dead man, dead under torture?—What is power to a
    man
Living, after the flesh is content?   Reason is never a
    root, neither of act nor desire.

For power living I would never do it; they are not
    delightful to touch, one wants to be separate.   For
    power
After the nerves are put away underground, to lighten
    the abstract unborn children toward peace . . .

A man might have paid anguish indeed.   Except he had
    found the standing sea-rock that even this last
Temptation breaks on; quieter than death but lovelier;
    peace that quiets the desire even of praising it.

VII

Yet look: are they not pitiable?   No: if they lived for-
    ever they would be pitiable:
But a huge gift reserved quite overwhelms them at the
    end; they are able then to be still and not cry.

And having touched a little of the beauty and seen a
    little of the beauty of things, magically grow
Across the funeral fire or the hidden stench of burial
    themselves into the beauty they admired,

Themselves into the God, themselves into the sacred
    steep unconsciousness they used to mimic
Asleep between lamp's death and dawn, while the last
    drunkard stumbled homeward down the dark street.

They are not to be pitied but very fortunate; they need
    no savior, salvation comes and takes them by force,
It gathers them into the great kingdoms of dust and
    stone, the blown storms, the stream's-end ocean.

With this advantage over their granite grave-marks, of
   having realized the petulant human consciousness
Before, and then the greatness, the peace: drunk from
   both pitchers: these to be pitied? These not fortu-
   nate?

But while he lives let each man make his health in his
   mind, to love the coast opposite humanity
And so be freed of love, laying it like bread on the
   waters; it is worst turned inward, it is best shot
   farthest.

Love, the mad wine of good and evil, the saint's and the
   murderer's, the mote in the eye that makes its
   object
Shine the sun black; the trap in which it is better to
   catch the inhuman God than the hunter's own image.

SOLILOQUY

August and laurelled have been content to speak for an
    age, and the ages that follow
Respect them for that pious fidelity;
But you have disfeatured time for timelessness.
They had heroes for companions, beautiful youths to
    dream of, rose-marble-fingered
Women shed light down the great lines;
But you have invoked the slime in the skull,
The lymph in the vessels. They have shown men Gods
    like racial dreams, the woman's desire,
The man's fear, the hawk-faced prophet's; but nothing
Human seems happy at the feet of yours.
Therefore though not forgotten, not loved, in gray old
    years in the evening leaning
Over the gray stones of the tower-top,
You shall be called heartless and blind;
And watch new time answer old thought, not a face
    strange nor a pain astonishing;
But you living be laired in the rock
That sheds pleasure and pain like hailstones.

BIRTH-DUES

Joy is a trick in the air; pleasure is merely contemptible,
    the dangled
Carrot that leads to market or precipice;
But limitary pain—the rock under the tower and the
    hewn coping
That takes thunder at the head of the turret—
Terrible and real. Therefore a mindless dervish carving
    himself
With knives will seem to have conquered the world.

The world's God is treacherous and full of unreason; a
    torturer, but also
The only foundation and the only fountain.
Who fights him eats his own flesh and perishes of
    hunger; who hides in the grave
To escape him is dead; who enters the Indian
Recession to escape him is dead; who falls in love with
    the God is washed clean
Of death desired and death dreaded.

He has joy, but joy is a trick in the air; and pleasure,
    but pleasure is contemptible;
And peace; and is based on solider than pain.
He has broken boundaries a little and that will estrange
    him; he is monstrous, but not
To the measure of the God. . . . But I having told
    you—

[187]

However I suppose that few in the world have energy
 to hear effectively—
Have paid my birth-dues; am quits with the people.

DAY AFTER TO-MORROW

Mourning the broken balance, the hopeless prostration
    of the earth
Under men's hands and their minds,
The beautiful places killed like rabbits to make a city,
The spreading fungus, the slime-threads
And spores; my own coast's obscene future: I remember
    the farther
Future, and the last man dying
Without succession under the confident eyes of the stars.
It was only a moment's accident,
The race that plagued us; the world resumes the old
    lonely immortal
Splendor; from here I can even
Perceive that that snuffed candle had something . . . a
    fantastic virtue,
A faint and unshapely pathos . . .
So death will flatter them at last: what, even the bald
    ape's by-shot
Was moderately admirable?

AFTERWORD

Robinson Jeffers has been a source of literary controversy since the publication of *Roan Stallion, Tamar and Other Poems* in 1925. He has been hailed as a prophet and cursed as a nihilist. His "tragic narratives" have been called a "unique contribution to our literature" and dismissed as "beneath critical notice."[1] Much of the controversy stems from Jeffers' insistence that man look beyond "humanity" to inhuman nature for the source of belief and conduct. In his poem *Roan Stallion*, Jeffers writes, "Humanity is the start of the race; I say/ Humanity is the mould to break away from, the crust to break through, the coal to break into fire,/The atom to be split."[2]

Some have viewed breaking human ties as an invitation to depravity. They cite the violence of certain Jeffers characters and Jeffers' eventual choice of the term "Inhumanism" to describe his attitude as proof of the dangers in his work. Others have seen Jeffers' insistence that man "break away" as a call to see nature as the

1. Frederic I. Carpenter, *Robinson Jeffers* (New York: Twayne, 1962), p. 11. Sculley Bradley et al., *The American Tradition in Literature*, vol. 2, 4th ed. (New York: Grosset & Dunlap, 1974), p. 1213. See also Alex A. Vardamis, *The Critical Reputation of Robinson Jeffers: A Bibliographical Study* (Hamden, Conn.: Archon Books, 1972).

2. Robinson Jeffers, *The Selected Poetry of Robinson Jeffers* (New York: Random House, 1938), p. 149.

religious meditation defined by Emerson in his essay "Nature" and explored by Thoreau at Walden Pond. Jeffers' descriptions show the justice of both views. At times he describes grand vistas of ocean, rock, or sunset, inviting his reader to "reject" "human solipsism" and accept "the transhuman magnificence."[3] Other times, Jeffers portrays a nature of predators and violence, arguing that pain and impermanence are the order of life and that one must at times be cruel to survive and win through to vision.

The Inhumanist, especially the Inhumanist poet, must reconcile the dichotomy between nature as a source of grace and nature as an experience of violent destruction. At the same time, the Inhumanist must transcend his human perspective and confront nature without denying what Jeffers recognizes is the source of his "natural" identity: his humanness. The Inhumanist must not love solipsistically or regard himself with contempt. Jeffers writes:

> Yet I am the one made pledges against the refuge contempt, that easily locks the world out of doors.
> This people as much as the sea-granite is part of the God from whom I desire not to be fugitive.[4]

We must be human and in-human. We must worship "organic wholeness" and "not man apart from that"[5]

3. Robinson Jeffers, *The Double Axe and Other Poems* (New York: Liveright, 1977), p. vii.

4. Jeffers, *Selected Poetry,* p. 202. See also the section of short poems at the end of this edition, where "Meditation on Saviors" is reprinted under its original title, "Note on 'The Women at Point Sur.'"

5. *Selected Poetry,* p. 594.

(nor that apart from man). Jeffers' concern with balancing man's relation to nature and to man suggests that Inhumanism should be approached less as a philosophic code than a religious injunction to confront certain contradictions and tensions. The violent actions of a narrative like *The Women at Point Sur* are a strategy for awakening poet and reader to the conflicts of being human and in nature. Poems like *Point Sur* seek to lead poet and reader to attain moments of vision and "organic wholeness" with the "transhuman magnificence."

The sensational plot of *The Women at Point Sur* seems at first anything but religious. The story opens with the Reverend Arthur Barclay renouncing his pulpit and declaring to his congregation that "Christianity is false." Barclay then wanders off along the Sur coast to, as he puts it, "break through" to the "power behind appearances." Like Melville's Ahab, who also would "strike through the mask," Barclay chooses to risk blasphemy in order to seize God and know his purposes. Also like Ahab, Barclay brings destruction on himself and those around him. As *Point Sur* progresses, Barclay increasingly confuses his search for the "power behind appearances" with his own desire for personal power and gratification. He gathers disciples to "hurl against God" and declares himself the prophet of a new order "beyond good and evil." Under his self-declared dispensation, Barclay countenances various adulteries and infanticide, blesses the homosexual union of two women, and rapes his twenty-year-old daughter. Eventually, Barclay encourages his followers to an orgy that culminates in the nightmare-like rebirth of a crippled, elderly farmer, the death of Barclay's deranged daughter, who shoots herself believing that she is her dead brother come to avenge her rape (Barclay at points also confuses his identity with that of his dead son), and Barclay's own death in the desert. The poem closes with Barclay's deluded proclamation, "I am inexhaustible."

When the poem was published in June 1927, critical reaction was largely negative. Those friendly to Jeffers claimed that the poem bogged down in its own convoluted plot. Others condemned the poem as hysterical and immoral. Publicly, Jeffers said little. Privately, however, he attempted to justify the poem. In a letter to his friend James Rorty, Jeffers claimed that a primary "intention" of *Point Sur*

> . . . was to show in action the danger of that "Roan Stallion" idea of "breaking out of humanity," misinterpreted in the mind of a fool or a lunatic. . . . It is not anti-social, because it has nothing to do with society; but just as Ibsen in the Wild Duck made a warning against his own idea in the hands of a fool, so Point Sur was meant to be a warning; but at the same time a reassertion.[6]

Jeffers is right to point out that Barclay is deluded and that his career is a destructive parody of the Inhumanist attempt to go beyond humanity, but the claim that Barclay's quest is both "warning" and "reassertion" fails to clarify Barclay's claim that he is "inexhaustible." Barclay's career *is* fundamentally ambiguous, and Jeffers' letter to Rorty does little more than rationalize the ambiguity. It does not clarify whether the ambiguity is meaningful or simply a reflection of Jeffers' own confusion.

6. Ann N. Ridgeway, *The Selected Letters of Robinson Jeffers: 1897–1962* (Baltimore: Johns Hopkins Press, 1968), p. 116.

In a letter written while preparing the final copy for publication, Jeffers confided to Donald Friede, his editor at Liveright, that *Point Sur* is "—I dare say—the Faust of this generation."[7] This is a much stronger statement than Jeffers ever cared to make for *Point Sur* after its negative public reception, and it suggests that Jeffers' hopes for the poem were more positive than the conservative moral exemplum expressed to Rorty. It also suggests that it is necessary to look beyond Barclay's career to understand the poem. In the basic Faust story, Faust sells his soul to the devil in order to gain knowledge and experience. According to the particular version, Faust is finally damned to hell as the price of his insight or led by his insight to come back to God, who forgives and saves him. In one sense, Barclay fits the Faustian model. For the sake of knowledge, he willingly risks his own damnation. Unlike Faust, Barclay never attains insight. He begins his career claiming to his congregation that he and they are "blind," and he dies equally blind. Where, then, is the insight that should come from the violence and degradation of Barclay's career? It is with the poet and, secondarily, the reader. To understand the Faustian dimensions of *Point Sur,* it is necessary to focus on the narrator and his stake in the story he creates and not on Barclay, the protagonist.

In the "Prelude" that introduces the narrative of Barclay, Jeffers writes, "discovery's/ The way to walk in. Only remains to invent the language to tell it." Here, Jeffers refers to the discovery that is to be his in writing the poem and the discovery that is to be the reader's in reading it. In a sense, Jeffers introduces Barclay's story by instructing himself and his reader that Barclay's

7. *Selected Letters,* p. 105.

quest is secondary to their own and by implying that *Point Sur,* in spite of its elaborate plot, is something other than a narrative poem. It is important, then, for the reader of the poem to understand how this first-person meditation controls the narrative that follows, how Jeffers defines his own stake in his storytelling, and how the poet and story interact to form a poem that fuses lyric and narrative elements.

"Prelude" is composed of three distinct units. The first, the first twenty-one verses, was printed originally in the *American Mercury* under the title "Preface."[8] It summarizes what the rest of the poem explores at greater length.

> When the animals Christ was rumored to have died
>   for drew in,
> The land thickening, drew in about me, I planted
>   trees eastward, and the ocean
> Secured the west with the quietness of thunder. I
>   was quiet.
> Imagination, the traitor of the mind, has taken my
>   solitude and slain it.
> No peace but many companions; the hateful-eyed
> And human-bodied are all about me.

The images imply that the poet's "solitude" has been "slain" by the people drawing in, but the central sentence states directly that the poet's own "imaginaton" is to blame. In a sense, the conflict is only apparent, since it is the "human-bodied" who trigger the poet's imagination. But in another sense, this link only intensifies the problem; the poet, too, is one of the "human-

8. S. S. Alberts, *A Bibliography of the Works of Robinson Jeffers* (New York: Random House, 1933), pp. 37, 40.

[196]

bodied," and what he shares with the crowd makes him vulnerable to their influence. The Inhumanist perspective suggests one explanation of the poet's situation. In these lines, he finds that he is all too human in the negative sense. Rather than having broken beyond humanity and transcended his contradictory self, he has simply withdrawn and attempted to ignore. He has succumbed to the temptation of contempt that locks out "the God from whom I desire not to be fugitive."

The poet's uneasiness about his humanity is further complicated by his role of poet. From lamenting his slain solitude, the poet shifts directly to the central question,

> But why should I make fables again? There are
>   many
> Tellers of tales to delight women and the people.
> I have no vocation. The old rock under the house,
>   the hills with their hard roots and the ocean
>   hearted
> With sacred quietness from here to Asia
> Make me ashamed to speak . . .

Jeffers' uneasiness with making fables is twofold. The fable claims to instruct and to know truth. The poet feels that his own human conflicts make him unable to play the role of fablemaker; he fears that the frailty that allows the crowd to excite his imagination will lead him to misuse his language and audience. In addition, he doubts the ability of his audience to profit even were he capable of embodying truth in fable. This may seem an odd concern, but the success of *Roan Stallion, Tamar and Other Poems* was of a sort to trouble Jeffers. The sensationalistic elements of the two title poems, double incest in one and hints of sodomy in the other, had com-

[197]

bined with the image of the solitary poet in his stone house overlooking the Pacific to captivate the imagination of the Roaring Twenties. Critics praised, religious leaders condemned the "pagan terror," and tyro writers stalked the campuses with Gibran's *The Prophet* under one arm and *Roan Stallion* under the other. By the time Jeffers was writing *Point Sur,* he was rapidly becoming a cult figure and might well be uneasy that the religious vision behind his injunction to "break away" from humanity was being obscured by public enthusiasm for his personal image.

At the simplest level, the conflict for Jeffers is between his identity as a religious seeker and his desire to be a religious teacher. As one seeking to overcome personal impurity, he feels, despite his slanders of the "hateful-eyed," the call to spread the truth. At the same time, he mistrusts his impulse to preach because his vision enjoins him to leave humanity behind, and he fears that preaching may be just another facet of the tie to humanity he needs to transcend. As one who seeks truth, the poet almost by definition, does not possess it. He doubts not only the rightness of his impulse to teach but also the truth of what he has to teach. Jeffers fears that his own impurity will lead him into false prophecy and into a search for power in order to compensate for his inadequacy before "God" and "the universe."

If Jeffers were writing within an orthodox religious framework, his problem of insight and authority would be solved by the presence of a sacred text. His job would be to interpret and propagate. But Jeffers is enough of an Emersonian and romantic to believe that religious experience is inherently personal, that each individual must search for and experience grace for himself. Walt Whitman's "Song of Myself" suggests one poetic strategy in response to this Emersonian perspective. In "Song of Myself," there are two presences that go under the name of "Walt." The one generally discussed is an idealization of Whitman, a prophet figure who transcends space and time claiming to "launch all men and women forward with me into the Unknown." Throughout the poem, though, Whitman asserts that this prophetic Walt Whitman, this "kosmos, of Manhattan the son," is a "performer" imagined by the Walt Whitman who shares with his reader the same ordinary human dimensions and mortality. It is this everyday Walt Whitman who admits that it would be a "mistake" to imagine that one "could forget the mockers and insults!" Without the presence of the everyday Walt Whitman, the Walt as vulnerable to death as his readers, Whitman could not assert what is the Emersonian key to the poem: that all can rise to the same visionary heights. Whitman's insistence that his visions are open to all leads him in the course of "Song of Myself" to undercut his own poem, and, seven lines from the end, he asserts, "If you want me again look for me under your boot-soles."

Although Whitman clearly aspires to prophecy in "Song of Myself," the prophecy hoped for is one that in the last analysis would disappear, leaving the reader launched on his own search for vision. Whitman convinces of the need to seek vision by embodying and demonstrating his own search for vision in the form of the poem. Likewise, in *Point Sur*, Jeffers responds to the conflict between religious seeking and teaching by asserting that he and his readers are mutually involved in discovery through the provisional medium of the poem.

> Culture's outlived, art's root-cut, discovery's
> The way to walk in.   Only remains to invent the
>   language to tell it.   Match-ends of burnt ex-
>   perience
> Human enough to be understood,
> Scraps and metaphors will serve.

In "Song of Myself," Whitman establishes the provisional nature of the poem by contrasting the everyday Walt and the Walt of vision.   Whitman catches his reader in the movement from one Walt to the other and back again.   In *The Women at Point Sur,* Jeffers establishes the poem's provisional nature by insisting that the reader follow the interaction between the poet and the story he creates.   In the first section of "Prelude," Jeffers alerts his reader that the poem is offered not as "fable" but as an attempt at "discovery," that the story of Barclay does not embody or illustrate preconceived truth but searches for truth.   At its most basic, the first section of "Prelude" functions as a warning, telling the reader that what is to come is not a tale to delight or a tale to instruct.   It tells the reader that the narrator claims no insight beyond that possessed by his reader.   Rather, he informs his reader that he will proceed to fashion a narrative out of his own confusions and inner tensions and that he will then do his best to use that narrative to discover a way beyond his confusions.

The process of discovery begins in the second section of "Prelude."   According to Sidney Alberts, "Prelude" originally began with what is now verse twenty-two,

"Come storm, kind storm," and what follows is essentially the poet's invocation of his muse.

> Come storm, kind storm.
> Summer and the days of tired gold
> And bitter blue are more ruinous.
> The leprous grass, the sick forest,
> The sea like a whore's eyes,
> And the noise of the sun,
> The yellow dog barking in the blue pasture,
> Snapping sidewise.

In these lines there are several storms: a storm remembered and a storm hoped for; the storm of nature and the storm of the imagination. On one level, Jeffers is invoking the storm that will end the late-summer California dry season, the rains that will cut the heat and end the danger of range and forest fires. On a personal level, Jeffers parallels his own situation to that of the land. He accuses himself of having become "tired and corrupt." "You kept the beast under till the fountain's poisoned." He desires a storm that will purge: the storm of the poem. He addresses his reader, his characters, and himself:

> . . . to each of you at length a little
> Desolation; a pinch of lust or a drop of terror:
> Then the lions hunt in the brain of the dying: storm
>   is good, storm is good, good creature,
> Kind violence, throbbing throat aches with pity.

This storm figuratively gathers the imaginative, emotional, and physical elements. Storm is "kind" because its purgation is as natural and necessary as the change of seasons. To avoid it is to resort to something similar

[201]

to contempt and risk the violence of fire instead of the violence of "running clouds and the iron wind." By analogy, Jeffers' poem will function like the necessary purgation of storm. It will court violence in order to release the inner tensions while they can still, it is hoped, be controlled and turned toward transcendence and vision rather than annihilation. "Prelude's" second section establishes the thematic breadth and importance of "storm," and it suggests that the process of discovery will take place through the poet's imaginative purgation. It also shows the poet functioning as a dramatic character for the first time. The invocation of storm reads like a dramatic soliloquy.

The third and final section of "Prelude" is the first to introduce a narrative voice, and it is in this section that Jeffers establishes his involvement with the characters of his narrative. The passage is an extended description of storm and the strain it evokes.

> . . . The lighthouse-keeper believes in hell,
> His daughter's wild for a lover, his wife sickening
>   toward cancer,
> The long yellow beam wheels over the wild sea and
>   the strain
> Gathers in the air.

The phrase, "the strain," is repeated through the entire section.

> The strain in the skull, blind strains, force and
>   counter-force,
> Nothing prevails . . .

Strain is univesal in the world of the poem. The characters are caught by the strain of their emotional confusions; the oil in the storage tanks at Monterey strains to burn and release the energy compressed in its molecules. Only one element avoids being driven by the strain revealed by storm, a hawk, and this hawk keys the poet's meditation and the parallel meditation of the character Onorio Vasquez, a "young seer of visions." His brothers have winged the hawk and "crucified" it on the barn wall. Both Onorio and the poet look to the hawk as if it might explain the chaos of storm. Both focus on the hawk's eyes and feel that the inscrutable hawk somehow contains and yet transcends the strain of his condition. Finally, the poet asks Onorio:

Don't you see any vision Onorio Vasquez? "No,
    for the topazes
Have dulled out of his head, he soars on two nails,
Dead hawk over the coast.

Faced with the now dead hawk, Onorio pleads with his brother to nail him to the barn door, explaining, " 'It is necessary for someone to be fastened with nails./ And Jew-beak died in the night.' "

The hawk that "flies on two nails" with "great eyes" functions in several ways. It suggests the purgation and transcendence of the Inhumanist perspective. Also, it helps define the role of the Inhumanist artist as the one who would be "fastened with nails," imaginatively at least, in order to provoke vision. Finally, the overlapping meditations of Onorio and the poet triggered by the hawk clarify the relationship of the lyric, confessional elements of "Prelude" and the narrative elements of Barclay's story. The response of Onorio and the poet to the hawk is so similar that their meditations are in effect a single meditation. Only quotation marks distinguish the character's speech from that of the poet. The character has a dramatic identity of his own, but, in the presence of the hawk, poet and character merge and remain merged until the hawk's death, when the poet questions, "Don't you see any vision Onorio Vasquez?" Onorio's response answers the question but indirectly to another character. When Onorio asks his brother to crucify him in place of the hawk, the poet agrees that an image of suffering is needed but disagrees with the literalistic strategy. Jeffers' relationship with Onorio follows a simple pattern: he creates the character, merges with and experiences through him, and then withdraws to interpret and judge the experience. The same pattern governs Jeffers' relationship with *Point Sur*'s main character, Barclay. He creates the character, merges, and separates. This changing relationship between character and poet, not the plot, is the key to *Point Sur*'s structure, and to follow it profitably, the reader must shift his attention from the significance of the story to the significance of the poet's involvement, his dramatic interaction, with the story he creates.

The first eleven sections of the narrative, roughly the first third of *Point Sur,* establish the character of Barclay, and the relationship of Barclay and the poet is consistently that of character and narrator. There are, of course, important similarities between Barclay and the figure of the poet established in "Prelude." Both, for instance, are religious seekers who suffer from having no vocation. However, Barclay, unlike the poet, eventually confuses his search for truth with the search for power and turns disastrously to gather disciples. In Barclay, Jeffers creates a character who succumbs to what he fears is his own weakness: a predilection for the pleasures of disciples. In this sense, Barclay's story is the

[204]

cautionary tale described to Rorty, but the poet and not the reader is the one cautioned.

The merger of Barclay and the poet is signaled in section XIII, when Jeffers interrupts the story to question the poem's direction.

> I made glass puppets to speak of him, they splintered
>   in my hand and have cut me, they are heavy
>   with my blood. . . .
> I sometime
> Shall fashion images great enough to face him
> A moment and speak when they die.   These here
>   have gone mad: but stammer the tragedy you
>   crackled vessels.

Frederic Carpenter has characterized this passage as a "clear-eyed admission of comparative failure."[9] It is, but Carpenter assumes that the admission applies to the poem as a whole.   Rather, it refers to the traditional narrative of the first eleven sections.   Although Carpenter feels that these early sections achieve "moments of great power before the reassertion of Jeffers' idea degenerates into the 'lunatic' perversion of it," Jeffers sees them as the sort of fable criticized in "Prelude."

> Here were new idols again to praise him;
> I made them alive; but when they looked up at the
>   face before they had seen it they were drunken
>   and fell down.
> I have seen and not fallen, I am stronger than the
>   idols,
> But my tongue is stone how could I speak him?   My
>   blood in my veins is seawater how could it catch
>   fire?

9. Carpenter, pp. 72–75.

The characters' failure is, in one sense, no surprise. At least in the Old Testament, to look on the face of God is to die. The poet's failure is, perhaps, less clear but has to do with standing too aloof from the world of the poem. He too has risked blasphemy but then, in holding his characters at the arm's length of traditional fiction, attempted to cover his blasphemy and deny the "strain" of "Prelude."

The attempt at "breaking out" into "discovery" requires that the poet (and reader) risk imaginatively the same impiety and damnation that the characters risk, and this is what Jeffers does in admitting the extent to which Barclay's passions are his own and by allowing himself to participate completely in the storm of Barclay's imagination. The poet's relationship with Barclay and the sudden stocktaking of section XII is foreshadowed at the end of section XI, where Barclay debates with his "mirror-image." In the letter to Rorty, Jeffers writes:

> Barclay incited people to "be your desires . . . flame
> . . . enter freedom." The remnant of his sanity—if
> that was the image of himself that he met on the
> hilltop—asks him whether it is for love of mankind
> that he is "pouring poison in the little vessels?" He
> is forced to admit that if the motive seems love, the
> act is an act of hatred.

There is a certain coyness in "if that was the image," and at one point, when the image says to Barclay, "I listened all the while with secret laughter/ The time we persuaded ourself we wanted disciples to bait the God-trap," the plural-singular "ourself" refers as easily to Jeffers regarding Barclay as a part of himself as to Barclay and his own projection. Section XII recalls the issues and ambience of "Prelude." It signals the shift away from conventional narrative. To make the "seawater" in his "veins . . . catch fire," the poet realizes he must confront his relationship to Barclay. To do so, the poet merges with Barclay as with Onorio in "Prelude" and gives his unconscious full sway in spinning out the narrative. As a result, the narrative logic of *Point Sur* after section XII is increasingly that of dream. The plot becomes increasingly violent and perverse; characters' identities blur, break down, and shift. It might be said that after section XII, *Point Sur* is increasingly objective in its expression of increasingly subjective material.

Jeffers works to control the nightmare of *Point Sur's* last sections in two ways. One is the context established by "Prelude"; the poet's participation in Barclay's degeneration is the psychic storm prayed for in the beginning. Secondly, Jeffers uses rhetorical interjections to indicate moments where the poet struggles to order his experience or to emphasize the poet's emotional interaction with Barclay. At the bottom of page 97, Jeffers writes:

> I say that if the mind centers on humanity
> And is not dulled, but remains powerful enough to
>   feel its own and the others, the mind will go
>   mad. . . .

Here, caught in the painful storm of Barclay, the poet pulls back long enough to remind himself and his reader of the poem's purpose by echoing the argument of "Prelude." On page 106, "The strain, the strain in the air. Come lightning?" is an example of the second type of interjection. The line recalls the emotional strain of "Prelude's" third section, and, although no first-person pronoun labels this as the poet, neither do quotation marks establish that it is Barclay.

The poet's struggle to contain "the strain" and his gamble for "discovery" suggest that *Point Sur* is best read as a drama with the poet himself the focal character. The poem's conclusion underscores this. Barclay dies still caught in his own confusions while the poet, and through him the reader, resolve them (or accept them). Again, "Prelude's" ending clarifies the situation. Onorio's and the poet's response to the hawk's death is emotionally the same. Both believe in the necessity of suffering to discover and the necessity of a symbol of suffering to inspire the search for truth. However, the poet's understanding of these things at the end of the meditation outstrips that of his characters. Onorio would have his brother crucify him, while the poet proceeds to explore the possibility of suffering imaginatively and of creating imaginatively a symbol of suffering.

Similarly, at the end of *Point Sur,* the poet and Barclay share equivalent experiences, but the poet's insight transcends that of his character. In section XXXI, Barclay's world collapses. His followers die or drop away, and Barclay walks alone, "like a burnt pillar," into the desert, where he dies. Images of fire and ash abound. The destroying hero meets his destruction. The poet's world is also in collapse. His imaginative "bacchanal" has reduced the figures in the poem to mere "shells." The situation seems one of entropy and not transcendence or discovery. However, Barclay's speeches in the section reveal another dimension. They reveal a mind divided against itself. At one point, Barclay says, " '. . . think on the nothing/ Outside the stars, the other shore of me, there's peace.' " Barclay sees himself simultaneously as all and nothing. He emphasizes the "transhuman magnificence" but then solipsistically

claims identity with it. Likewise, Barclay asserts that
" 'pain's . . . the foundation,' " but then at another
moment, " 'I grow weary of discovery,' " the discovery
that issues from pain. Through suffering and destruc-
tion, Barclay has attained a degree of vision, but in the
process exhausted himself and is unable to hold to what
he has found.

Jeffers' awareness of Barclay's confusion is evident
in the careful juxtaposition of Barclay's statements and
in the use of physical details that both evoke and inter-
pret the situation. After Barclay's internal debate,
Jeffers writes, "He [Barclay] ran northward . . .
turned/ Away from the light . . . [and] Lay down in
the mouth of the black pit." Literally, the black pit is
the mouth of a coal mine, but it is also emblematic of the
despair to which Barclay has succumbed rather than face
his discovery that " 'pain's . . . the foundation.' "
Also, when Barclay turns from the light it is a literal
turning away. He turns from the setting sun to walk
inland, but figuratively Barclay turns from the truth,
lacking the strength to face what he has glimpsed.

The poet, however, does not turn from the truth. As
earlier with Onorio, he separates from Barclay, evoking
for himself and the reader a level of understanding
beyond the character's grasp. The dichotomy between
the poet and Barclay is implicit in the split in Barclay's
speech and the double nature of the descriptive details.
It is also implicit in Jeffers' use of images of ritual
sacrifice.[10] Ritual sacrifice is a common motif in Jeffers'

10. My discussion of the ritual aspect of *The Women at
Point Sur* is indebted to the work of Robert Brophy, *Robin-
son Jeffers: Myth, Ritual, and Symbol in His Narrative Poems*
(Cleveland: Case Western Reserve University Press, 1973),

[209]

long poems. In *Point Sur,* Barclay is often the sacrific-
ing priest. He justifies his rape of his daughter April as
a ritualistic violation of societal norms allowed a seeker
of truth. Likewise, Barclay brings his followers to
orgiastic frenzy to promote his quest for vision, and in
section XXXI, when Natalia Morhead's dead baby is
brought before him, Barclay instructs, as might a priest
of Dionysus, " 'hack her in pieces,/ For each a mouth-
ful.' "

Once Barclay leaves his followers behind in the second
half of section XXXI, the drift of the sacrificial imagery
shifts. Instead of being the one who sacrifices, Barclay
becomes the one sacrificed; instead of the priest, he is
the victim. Jeffers describes Barclay as "like a burnt
pillar/ Smeared with the blood of sacrifice." That
"pillar" is used earlier as a synonym for phallus intensi-
fies the sense of Dionysian or fertility ritual. Also, the
image of Barclay as a "burnt pillar" alone in the desert
echoes the pillar of fire that guides the Israelites, but
Barclay has reached a point of exhaustion and confusion.
Burnt out, he is finally and irrevocably a false prophet.
Barclay's last speech, the last lines of the poem, under-
scores his identity as a type or image of fertility god.

"I want creation. The wind over the desert
Has turned and I will build again all that's gone
    down.
I am inexhaustible."

That the wind has turned suggests the turn of the year
and, given the context, the ritual planting of the phallus

and William Everson (Brother Antoninus), *Robinson Jeffers:
Fragments of an Older Fury* (Berkeley: Oyez, 1968). Any
recent critic of Jeffers cannot help but be influenced by
Brophy's and Everson's work.

to ensure the return of fertility and spring. Death and rebirth coexist in the image of the sacrificial fertility god just as they do in a striking image from the previous page, where Barclay, having earlier "gathered up in his hands a heap of red coals," falls on his hands so that "the burnt palms cracked and blood ran down from the fingers." The life force flows from the ashes, perhaps just as "discovery" flows from "the foundation" of "pain." The sense of life within death is also suggested by Barclay's bleeding palms and his three days in the pit, details which echo the passion of Christ. Barclay is not, of course, a primitive fertility god able to be dismembered and healed annually any more than he is Christ. His death is final. His stay in the black pit leads to death, not resurrection.

It is the poet who experiences resurrection or rebirth in rising above the storm and strain of Barclay. At the end of the poem, it is the poet who is capable of looking "on the nothing/ Outside the stars," of admitting "the foundation" of "pain" and his "organic wholeness" with God without resorting to megalomania. In Barclay, Jeffers embodies the impurities and corruption of "Prelude" and allows them out of the "oubliette" into the light of consciousness. In Barclay's career, the poet confronts his personal image of damnation in order to burn through his conflicts and cast them aside. Through Barclay, the poet is able to evoke his own depravity and death and, paradoxically, in doing so attain a moment of vision of the "transhuman magnificence" and a moment of acceptance of his own death, his place in the flux of the universe. In this sense, it is the poet who has the right to exclaim, in recognizing his own life within death and death within life, " 'I am inexhaustible.' " The effect is similar to the ending of *Moby-Dick,* where the

[211]

destroying hero Ahab goes to his death while Ishmael is left to float, serenely buoyed to life on an empty sea by Queequeg's coffin. In the case of *Point Sur*, Barclay, like Ahab, embraces his death, and the poet, like Ishmael, rises above the death and hate. Ishmael and the poet participate in the blasphemies of their captain and hero, and both survive. It may even be that Jeffers' letter to Friede claiming *Point Sur* as the "Faust of this generation" reflects the same elation as Melville's boast to Hawthorne, "I have written a wicked book, and feel spotless as a lamb. . . . It is a strange feeling—no hopefulness is in it, no despair."

Ideally, the reader of *Point Sur* should also feel cleansed if he has allowed himself to identify with the poet, admit his own corruption, and face his need for purgation. *Point Sur,* like "Song of Myself" and even *Moby-Dick,* is a book that demands the reader's participation. It is a drama enacted and recorded so that the reader like the poet may renew himself periodically without finding himself trussed to a white whale or dying of thirst in a coal mine. The length and excesses of *Point Sur* must be understood as part of Jeffers' strategy to involve himself and his reader in "discovery." The poem is not meant to summarize the Inhumanist perspective but to involve the reader in the psychically volatile conflicts of being human and in the world so that the reader may, like the "you" in "Song of Myself," attain vision. As "Prelude" reveals, it is difficult to admit to the "strain" and the necessity of 'storm." In a letter to Rudolph Gilbert, Jeffers writes:

All the prevalent religions think of God as blessed, or happy, or at least at peace; even the pantheist mystic finds peace in God; therefore this conception of God as in pain is hardly admitted by the reader's mind. For this reason I built it up through the will-pointing of Prometheus, the self-hanging of Odin in Norse mythology, the personality of Gudrun, and the phantom of Christ, to make it poetically credible. It is a conception that runs through my verses, from "Heautontimor[o]umenos" (the self-tormentor) in "Women at Point Sur" (page 174) down to this latest. If God is all, he must be suffering, since an unreckoned part of the universe is always suffering. But his suffering must be self-inflicted, for he is all; there is no one outside him to inflict it.—I suppose the idea carries psychological as well as cosmic or religious implications. Man as well as God must suffer in order to discover; and it is often voluntary—self-inflicted—suffering.[11]

In his *ars poetica,* "Apology for Bad Dreams," written while Jeffers worked on the earliest versions of *Point Sur,* Jeffers writes:

"I bruised myself in the flint mortar and burnt me
In the red shell, I tortured myself, I flew forth,
Stood naked of myself and broke me in fragments,
And here am I moving the stars that are me."[12]

Jeffers would have his reader bruise himself in a "flint mortar" and discover "the stars" that are each of us. His long poems, by recording in dramatic form his own efforts at discovery, offer the reader a starting point for his own quest for discovery, his own attempt to evoke his own storm. The reader must confront himself and

11. *Selected Letters,* p. 240. In the edition of letters, the phrase "will-pointing" is printed as "wall-pointing." Ridgeway has recently concluded that her original reading was a misreading of Jeffers' script.
12. *Selected Poems,* p. 176.

search for his "organic wholeness" with the "trans-human magnificence." When *The Women at Point Sur* was first published fifty years ago, it was condemned for not being what it sought to avoid, a narrative, a "fable." Now, perhaps we are more ready to respond to poems like *Point Sur* that ask us to put ourselves on the line for our own sake.

TIM HUNT

TEXTUAL NOTE

The present text for *The Women at Point Sur* is based
on the original edition published by Boni & Liveright in
June 1927. All told, four changes have been made.
When Jeffers was correcting galley proofs for *Point Sur,*
Liveright asked for several changes. Earlier in 1927,
while Jeffers prepared the final typescript of the poem,
Donald Friede, his editor at Liveright, was convicted on
obscenity charges for distributing Theodore Dreiser's
An American Tragedy, and at the time Jeffers was
reading proof, hearings were being held in the New
York state legislature on an anti-obscenity bill.   To
avoid possible censorship, Jeffers obliged Liveright by
deleting several verses, replacing one, and substituting
the word "loved" for "stabbed."   This substitution was
on page 91, verse three.

The present edition restores the text to what seems
to have been Jeffers' original intention.   Although the
changes are perhaps not major, they clarify several im-
portant lines of imagery.   In addition to the change
described above, the other changes are as follows:

page 11, verse 21: "The shadow of hair under the belly,
    the jutting breasts like hills, the face in the hands
    and the hair" has been substituted for the 1927 edi-
    tion's "The heavy face hidden in the hands, the lips
    drinking the tears in the hollow hands and the hair".

page 17, verse 5: "The marriage bound thighs opening, on the stiff white straw, the nerves of fire, the ganglia like stars." was omitted from the 1927 edition.

page 165, verses 7 and 8: "Were a sword in our throats. They ought to have it cut off them/ When they're born, we'd be quieter. I wish that the rock" has been substituted for the 1927 edition's "Were a sword in our throats. I wish that the rock".

In each case, the galley proofs have been given authority over the 1927 edition. The galleys for *Point Sur* corrected in Jeffers' hand are located in the Beinecke Library, Yale University.

The other major change for the present edition of *The Women at Point Sur* is the inclusion of the five short poems. In his letters to Friede in early 1927, it is clear that Jeffers initially submitted six short poems to accompany the long narrative. All were eventually omitted, presumably because of space. As it stands, *The Women at Point Sur* is the only trade collection that Jeffers assembled that does not supplement the narrative with shorter lyrics.

Of the six poems submitted to Friede, four are named in the letters: "The Hurt Hawk," "Soliloquy," "Birth-Dues," and "Day after To-morrow." "Soliloquy" was included in *Cawdor,* published in 1928, and "Birth-Dues" in *Dear Judas,* published in 1929. "Day after To-morrow" eventually became Part V of "The Broken Balance" and was included in *Dear Judas.*[1] "The Hurt Hawk" as such was never published by Jeffers. In a letter to Friede on March 3, 1927, Jeffers writes:

1. See Alberts, *A Bibliography of the Works of Robinson Jeffers,* pp. 50, 56, 58.

Here is one more page for the monster [*Point Sur*]; I promise not to send any more. The title belongs in contents between "The Hurt Hawk" and "Soliloquy" . . .

I shot the hawk two days ago, and buried him in the courtyard.[2]

Since Part II of "Hurt Hawks" describes the shooting mentioned in the above letter and since the poem "The Hurt Hawk" had been submitted before the shooting, it seems likely that what was later printed as Part I of "Hurt Hawks" in *Cawdor* was originally entitled "The Hurt Hawk" and intended for inclusion in *The Women at Point Sur.*

The fifth poem added to the present edition appeared originally under the title *Meditation on Saviors* in *Cawdor.* However, the papers at Yale show that its original title was *Note on "The Women at Point Sur."* It is unclear whether the poem was finished in time for Jeffers to submit as part of the original manuscript of *Point Sur* or whether it was finished later and retitled because of *Point Sur's* negative public reception. In either case, it is a useful commentary on a difficult poem and has been included for that reason.

The text of the short poems corresponds to the text of *The Selected Poetry of Robinson Jeffers,* Random House, 1938, with two exceptions. Line two of "Birth-Dues" substitutes "that leads" for "the ass follows" and line eleven of "The Hurt Hawk" substitutes "power" for "one." In these two cases, the text followed is that of *Poems,* a collection of fifteen poems issued in 1928 by the Book Club of California. These versions are most

2. Ridgeway, *The Selected Letters of Robinson Jeffers: 1897–1962,* p. 107.

likely closest to the versions submitted to Boni & Liveright in 1927.

It should be noted that the short poems in the present edition are included primarily to provide the reader with material in support of *The Women at Point Sur.* The texts and titles followed have been chosen with that in mind and in no way are meant to replace or take precedence over their later form.

BIBLIOGRAPHICAL NOTE

Robinson Jeffers' major collections are *Roan Stallion, Tamar and Other Poems, The Women at Point Sur, Cawdor and Other Poems, Dear Judas and Other Poems, Thurso's Landing and Other Poems, Give Your Heart to the Hawks and Other Poems, Solstice and Other Poems, Such Counsels You Gave to Me and Other Poems, Be Angry at the Sun, The Double Axe and Other Poems, Hungerfield and Other Poems,* and *The Beginning and the End and Other Poems.* Many of these are out of print, but much of Jeffers' poetry is available in *The Selected Poetry of Robinson Jeffers* (Random House), *Cawdor and Medea* (New Directions), and *The Beginning and the End* (Random House). *The Women at Point Sur, Dear Judas,* and *The Double Axe* are all available from Liveright. Jeffers' letters have been edited by Ann Ridgeway and published under the title *The Selected Letters of Robinson Jeffers: 1897–1962* (Baltimore: Johns Hopkins Press, 1968). Bibliographies on Jeffers include S. S. Alberts, *A Bibliography of the Works of Robinson Jeffers* (published originally by Random House in 1933 and reissued in 1968 by Burt Franklin), and Alexander Vardamis, *The Critical Reputation of Robinson Jeffers: A Bibliographical Study* (Hamden, Connecticut: Archon Books, 1972). The one biography of Jeffers is Melba Berry Bennett, *The Stone Mason of Tor House: The Life and Work of Robinson Jeffers* (Los Angeles: Ward Ritchie Press, 1966). Another important source of bibliographical and biographical information is *Robinson Jeffers Newsletter,* published quarterly by Occidental College of Los Angeles.

Book-length studies of Jeffers include William Everson (Brother Antoninus), *Robinson Jeffers: Fragments of an Older Fury* (Berkeley: Oyez, 1968), Robert Brophy, *Robinson Jeffers: Myth, Ritual, and Symbol in His Narrative Poems* (Cleveland: Case Western Reserve University Press, 1973;

revised and reissued Hamden, Connecticut: Archon Press, 1976), Frederic I. Carpenter, *Robinson Jeffers* (New York: Twayne, 1962), Arthur B. Coffin, *Robinson Jeffers: Poet of Inhumanism* (Madison: University of Wisconsin Press, 1970), William Hotchkiss, *Robinson Jeffers: The Sivaistic Vision* (Auburn, California: Blue Oak Press, 1975), Lawrence Clark Powell, *Robinson Jeffers: The Man and His Work* (New York: Haskell, 1970; reissue of 1940 edition), and Radcliffe Squires, *The Loyalties of Robinson Jeffers* (Ann Arbor: University of Michigan Press, 1963). In addition to these studies, William Everson has edited three collections of Jeffers' earliest poems: *Californians, The Alpine Christ and Other Poems,* and *Brides of the South Wind: Poems 1917–1922.* All are published by Cayucos Books and include commentaries by Everson. These three volumes are particularly useful to those interested in tracing Jeffers' poetic development.